THE
Local
Church
SAYS
HELL, NO!

EARL PAULK
with Tricia Weeks

I wish to thank the Publications Department of Chapel Hill Harvester Church for their daily efforts and continuing dedication in the preparation of this book in the interest of communicating the gospel of the Kingdom of the Lord Jesus Christ.

I thank my Editorial Assistant, Tricia Weeks, for her capable contribution in writing and editing.

I thank Wes Bonner for his expertise in the coordination of publishing this book. I thank Angie Martin for editing and typesetting.

I deeply appreciate the volunteers who gave their time and skills to further the message of the Kingdom of God: Gloria Bassett for transcribing and Janis McFarland for proofreading.

May the seeds of these efforts bear much fruit to the glory of God.

Unless otherwise noted, all scripture quotations in this book are from **The New King James Version.**

Copyright 1991
Kingdom Publishers
Atlanta, Georgia

Printed in the United States of America
ISBN 0-917595-40-8

DEDICATION

Addie Mae Tomberlin Paulk
1907 - 1991

Y ou only have one mama. Mine was Addie Mae Tomberlin Paulk, one of a kind. She was a farmer's daughter and Granddaddy Tomberlin's favorite child. He never allowed Addie Mae to work under the hot sun in the fields. She stayed in the house cooking, and I reaped the benefits of all her childhood chores with "made from scratch" meals throughout my life.

She received the baptism of the Holy Spirit when she was only nine years old. She grew up in the Methodist church, but a traveling tent evangelist, S.J. Heath from Atlanta, held a Holy Ghost revival in Appling County. Mama became one of the first Pentecostals in the region. From a very young age, she could always touch God.

My Daddy preached the Word of God around the world and impacted the lives of thousands of people. As newlyweds, it was Addie Mae who taught her husband the Bible at night by the fire to compensate for his third-grade education.

She took being a wife and raising children as God's direct assignment to her. Mothering was her expertise. Even in the last few years of frail health, she would hold a doll close to her heart with the same tenderness as she had held her six babies.

She was responsible for much of the laughter in our home. She had a quick, sharp sense of humor, and never missed the slightest detail that deserved some witty commentary or correction.

Her eyes would flash, and we would all just get ready! I seldom needed to wonder what Mama thought at home. At church she was the perfect pastor's wife, keeping her thoughts discreetly to herself. She suffered too much from the criticism of church people to become a gossip.

She was a beautiful woman, and I was always so proud to be her son. I remember taking her shopping to J.C. Penney when I was about sixteen. She was trying on dresses, and I was offering her my opinion. The store clerk said to her, "You certainly have a young looking husband!" We laughed about that for years.

Because I was the eldest son left in charge while Daddy traveled the world, Mama gave me the responsibility of disciplining the younger children. If she had a headache, I was told to bring my younger brother Don to her bedside and spank him for her. She would coach, "Spank him some more; he isn't crying yet!"

I love her and will miss her as much as any son who has ever lived, but I wouldn't bring her back even if I could. I know she is enjoying talking with Joan, my sister, her own siblings who have gone before her, her parents and friends from the past. Most of all, I know how much she loves the Lord and will be totally at home in His presence.

I was especially grateful for friends from the Church of God who expressed their love and kindness to our family at Mama's death. Both Daddy and Mama gave their lives to serve God in that denomination.

Dr. Lewis J. Willis and Dr. Cecil Knight shared in Mama's

homegoing service at Chapel Hill Harvester Church with comments that would have pleased Mama so much! She loved the Church of God, and the roots of ministry in the lives of all my family members go deep into the history of those great churches.

In 1985 God took my baby sister Joan to be with Him on Pentecost Sunday. This year, 1991, the Lord spoke to me that the time between Easter and Pentecost Sunday would be a time of settling some things in my ministry. God told me to expect both great warfare and great blessings.

The year of someone's death marks something significant in the life of those who love that person. Like Isaiah, I would like to say, "In the year that Addie Mae died . . ." I'm not sure what words follow that phrase, but I know it signifies something great that God intends to do. Whatever it is, I know "I will see the Lord" in it, and I also know that Mama is cheering me on!

Our King Cometh!
Bishop Earl Paulk

FOREWORD

I find it very interesting that when God begins to stir a pastor's heart with a burden for cities, working at City Hall in that pastor's own hometown is a mayor of Christian conviction, integrity and character. Mayor Maynard Jackson represents good government that deserves the backing of Atlanta's local churches, and the fuel of Christians' involvement in creating quality living in our communities.

Mayor Jackson is the son and grandson of Baptist ministers. His great-great-grandfather, Andrew Jackson, a former slave who bought his own freedom, founded the Wheat Street Baptist Church in Atlanta. That heritage of service led Maynard Jackson into politics on April 8, 1968—the day Martin Luther King was buried and Maynard Jackson's first child was born.

In 1974, at age 35, Maynard Jackson became the youngest mayor in Atlanta's history, as well as the first black mayor of a major Southern city and of an American state capital. He was elected for a second term as mayor which began in 1990. He is a great leader with a great future, and my prayers are with him.

Bishop Earl Paulk

B ishop Earl Paulk is a spiritual father in a dynamic city that exemplifies all the greatness and challenges of modern society. Atlanta enjoys a rich heritage of working to build a community that demonstrates human equality and opportunity. Atlanta's mighty spiritual impact on the world is attributed to what I call an Atlanta "style." The Civil Rights movement captured that style by stirring the conscience of people everywhere to realize that a society that advocates justice and freedom must first respect the rights of all its citizens.

The Atlanta style is demonstrated by hard-working, church-going men and women who are willing to take their convictions into the streets to address problems directly and to make a difference in people's lives. I have seen such a commitment in Bishop Paulk and the ministry of Chapel Hill Harvester Church. Their work in public housing communities, AIDS clinics, drug rehabilitation, family counseling and youth ministry is contributing to the present and future strength of our city.

As mayor of Atlanta, I am especially grateful for the prayers and support I can always count on from Atlanta's spiritual leaders and Bishop Paulk in particular. We share the same goals for our city. Together we are called to serve people. That dedication to service that I recognize in those called by God into the ministry inspires me to fulfill my own calling to serve people through government.

I always say that people either live in Atlanta or wish they did. The truth is that Atlanta is representative of notable achievements and perils facing any metropolitan area around the world. I firmly believe that the willingness of Atlanta's citizens and leaders to find solutions to the problems we face can provide both hope and patterns for other cities facing turbulent times, rapid growth and political and economic struggles.

By knowing well the fruit of his ministry, I am very honored to recommend Bishop Paulk's book, **The Local Church Says, "Hell, No!"** His understanding of the responsibility of the Church in creating solutions for their community problems is commendable. Bishop Paulk teaches that words must translate into action. The relevance of his gospel in the service of Christian people is a tremendous asset to the mayor of Atlanta, Georgia, and to the citizens of this great city.

Mayor Maynard Jackson, Atlanta, Georgia

TABLE OF CONTENTS

1 Meet Your Enemy

I awoke from a very disturbing dream. In a restless sleep I had searched through the streets of a devastated city for the Presbytery of Chapel Hill Harvester Church in Atlanta. In my hand I clutched notes of a message that I desperately wanted to give them, but aimlessly I wandered about, trying to find the place of our meeting.

I walked into a public building resembling a post office to discover school rooms in total disarray with unsupervised children running wildly. Someone told me that the Presbytery might be meeting on the third floor. I waited for an elevator, but when the elevator door opened, the elevator was suspended several feet higher than the floor. Needless to say, I didn't take that elevator.

Outside, traffic in the shambled city moved only in narrow alleys because the main streets were cluttered with debris. Mobs of people gathered everywhere, most of them speaking in foreign languages. Their faces were drawn, distraught and hopeless, reflecting the devastation surrounding them.

I entered an old house to see a group of people gathered around a girl who had disrobed. I recognized several people in the group, and alarmed at seeing them, I asked, "What are you doing?"

"We're worshipping, Bishop," they answered. One of the young men broke away from the group and came to me. He offered to help me find the Presbytery.

Back in the streets, I spotted my son-in-law Sam, one of our pastors, driving by in a dilapidated green Volkswagen. Sam slowed down long enough for me to get inside the car through a window, and I noticed the car had two steering wheels—one for the driver and one for the front seat passenger—but mine didn't seem to steer the car. Sam and I searched for the rest of the Presbytery without finding them.

We drove through woods on dirt paths, dodging trees on both sides; we saw a group of farmers who had lost their crops; we saw people standing along the road as if they wanted to help us, but couldn't. I kept noticing church steeples towering over the city. Every time I looked at the steeples, a voice spoke in my spirit, "That is the reason this city is in such chaos."

One of the most frightening details of the dream was that I kept noticing that people we passed were putting something in their mouths and chewing on it. At last I realized that they were

2

eating money. I felt such panic as I awoke from the nightmare. I understood many of the symbols in the dream completely, but much of the content puzzled me.

The next day the Presbytery met with me for our regular Friday morning session, and I shared the dream with them. For quite some time God had been leading us to address many of the problems in Atlanta—public housing, drugs, AIDS, zoning issues, community development, inner city polarization along racial, economic and social lines. The content of the dream was not surprising in that regard, but we agreed God wanted us to understand with greater awareness the spiritual dimension of our city's problems.

Spiritual leaders need to have clear vision today. Many times we have a general direction, but we need a second touch from the Lord to see with clarity from God's perspective.

Then He came to Bethsaida; and they brought a blind man to Him, and begged Him to touch him. So He took the blind man by the hand and led him out of the town. And when He had spit on his eyes and put His hands on him, He asked him if he saw anything. And he looked up and said, "I see men like trees, walking." Then He put His hands on his eyes again and made him look up. And he was restored and saw everyone clearly. And He sent him away to his house, saying, "Neither go into the town, nor tell anyone in the town." (Mark 8:22-26)

I'm not certain of the reasons that Jesus led the blind man out of town to heal him. Perhaps the man needed to leave his circumstances in order for his faith to ignite. The guarded way that Jesus performed miracles is perhaps another reason He led the man away from the crowds. It's also interesting that Jesus spit directly into the man's eyes rather than making clay as He did in another instance. But the most interesting part of this story is that this healing consisted of two specific parts in order for the man to regain his sight fully.

I believe that many Christians today are beginning to see the world with spiritual vision from experiencing Jesus' touch upon their eyes. In our ministry in Atlanta we are experiencing a tremendous revival among young families—many of whom came to the church a decade ago as teenagers through a move called *Alpha*. After a season of some of these young converts cooling off in their Christian zeal, many have re-ignited with a fresh burst of God's fire.

Revival is breaking out all around the world, yet some believers still see what God is doing as if people with needs in their communities were trees, walking. They know vaguely what God wants them to do, but they need another touch from the Lord to receive full understanding. They don't yet grasp the full scope of God's plan and how they fit into it.

The second touch may surprise you. At the same time that victories are shouted from the housetops with great fanfare— the blind can see—God wants you to get the full picture in vivid detail. In order to do that, you need to meet your enemy. Unless you meet him, the fires of anointing will be extinguished before they can ever spread with the breadth and power that God intends for your life.

Why is this understanding necessary? If you do not meet your enemy, you will give up in the middle of battle. You will fail to understand that the impossible challenges you face in the near future are going to turn around for your benefit. Some people will lose jobs because God wants to place them in better jobs. Some people will lose what they thought were good relationships because God wants them to experience covenant relationships centered upon His purposes for their lives. Some people standing at the door of matrimony will realize that God was not the author of those plans at all. He has another way.

Unless you meet the enemy, and allow God to touch your eyes once more, you are going to be surprised, depressed and confused by the events in your life in the next few months. You'll think, "God, what is happening?" At the very time you are ready to give up and give in, God has prepared you for your greatest hour of witness for Him. You will miss the victories of abundant living unless you meet your enemy!

Who is your enemy? He is Lucifer. Lucifer was created by God as the most beautiful of the archangels, given a position of leadership in praise and worship before God. Because of pride leading to his rebellion against God, he was cast down to the earth. He is also called "Satan" and "the devil." Although he can never win the final battle, he assumes the role of God's chief opponent and man's chief adversary.

A television news magazine program, "20/20" on the ABC network, recently covered a story about the deliverance of someone from demon possession. In follow-up interviews for two days after that broadcast, experts were debating the topic, "Is there such a being as the devil?" Many of those experts in religion and psychology sort of laughed at the assertion and side-stepped stating their convictions—if they had any.

Get straight in your mind that if a personal God exists, a personal devil is also real. He has personality and free will. We know a great deal about him and the way he operates, but he knows much more about you and me. And he knows more about God than we do.

The devil is more disciplined than you are. He stays within his guidelines with more respect than you or I do when we are told by God where the boundaries are. I know this seems strange, but the devil takes orders from God better than you or I. He comprehends God's authority far more completely than we do.

The devil is the head of a major religion. He has a throne room all his own. He has synagogues within every religion, including some so-called Christian churches with beautiful buildings and respectable reputations.

I am not referring to satanism, per se. Most of the attention-getting antics that people use to get public attention as satanists are laughable to the real devil. He uses kids with weird haircuts, crazy clothes and drug addictions as a smokescreen to his real strategy. Those representing the sensational occult religions make the average citizens feel like they are safe from satanic activities. Wrong!

Wearing skeleton tee-shirts and chanting in rituals may destroy those involved in overt satanistic practices, and I am not understating the seriousness of blood sacrifices and the occult. But satanism is not the focus of Satan's activities in the world today. The truth is shocking as well as sobering. Satan is aware of you and much closer to you and your family than you realize.

The devil is a chief executive officer. He walks straight and tall. He has fire in his eyes just as Jesus is described as having in the Revelation. Satan loves power, and he is not afraid to use it. He is a commander with an army under his direction. One-third of all angelic forces listened to him and chose his leadership over

God's.

———————— **SATAN'S STRATEGY AND GOALS** ————————

Satan is a leader with strategy and goals. What are his goals?
He intends to unseat and overthrow God. He has experienced
what he considers to be a temporary loss with the resurrection
of Jesus Christ, but he has not even begun to concede the final
victory to God. While he sees the end in sight and knows the
battle will not rage forever, he has deceived himself into
believing—and fighting—as if he will win.

Jesus dealt Satan a heavy blow at Calvary, but the battle continues. Why does God allow it to continue? Jesus was "the first-
fruit of many brethren." The Church has an assignment of witnessing the gospel of the Kingdom to all nations—then the end
will come (Matthew 24:14). So Satan intends to stop that witness. He challenges God's authority in every respect—not only
in the universe, but also in your life.

Have you ever wondered why rebellious people hate men and
women of God? Ask yourself why it is that godly men and
women are ridiculed by the media and by unscrupulous people
in places of authority. Why do bold Christians make some people feel so threatened?

People who trust God and those who rebel against God do
not live in the same dimension. Ungodly people have an uncontrollable desire to attack those who belong to God. Just as they
attacked Jesus' reputation and verbally abused Him, people
under Satan's control will react against the Spirit of Christ in
you. The demoniac rushed toward Jesus to physically attack
Him, but the power of God restrained the man until Jesus deli-

from the demons.

ise, people under the devil's control want to attack good pec, e, and they don't even know the reasons. These destructive forces sometimes control people who love you and may have helped you at other times, but now they want to tear you apart. They are subjects of a totally different rule than you are.

Satan's goal today is to destroy God's plan of recovery. God's plan has always been for people under His rule to have children and to subdue the earth. But now most of mankind struggles merely to survive. Only people alive with the Spirit of God have the power to crush Satan's head—or rule. That is the reason Satan works so diligently at undermining and discrediting Christian authority. The authority within us—ministering in Jesus' name—is Satan's greatest threat.

Satan plans to prostitute God's creation by separating man from God. Satan seeks praise and worship just as God desires for us to enter into His presence with thanksgiving and praise. How do people praise Satan? In music. In dance. In social activities. You praise him every time you decide to follow his plan instead of God's.

Satan is a master strategist. What is his strategy? Satan deceives people through lies. Jesus said that the devil is a liar, and the father of lies (John 8:44). He can deceive people by making them feel as if they are the only ones who are right, while everyone else is wrong. But remember, God allows him to operate through lies. He will always remain within the limitations that God allows him.

Satan's strategy is to kill, steal and destroy (John 10:10). He tried to kill Moses as a baby because God had heard Israel's cries for a deliverer. He tried to kill Jesus from birth. Satan used

Herod's decree to kill all male children under three years old in order to wipe out the one male child who might be the Messiah.

Throughout Jesus' ministry, Satan tried to kill Him. Satan tried to kill Jesus after He had fasted forty days in the wilderness. Satan attempted to kill Him in raging storms on the sea with His disciples. The demoniac under Satan's control rushed out of the tombs toward Jesus, gnashing his teeth, ready to devour Jesus. Crowds tried to stone Him numerous times, but Jesus always walked away.

Jesus' death on the cross was Satan's greatest mistake. Though the dark, evil potentate believed he had won at last by crucifying Jesus, the Son of God became a willing sacrifice to pay the price of sin.

Satan may have originally believed he trapped Jesus, but the devil felt the sting of defeat quickly. Jesus had willingly given up His spirit. The grave could not hold the King of kings and Lord of lords. The devil has lived under the sentence of total defeat since that day.

Just as the devil focused all his forces upon killing Jesus, the forces of hell today are focused upon stopping the witness of the Church. The bottom line is who's in charge of Christians individually and corporately. Who rules your life? Who directs the leadership of your church?

Satan is a shameless thief who attempts to steal every promise God has ever spoken to your heart. God's promises to you are held in the hope realm—that incorruptible place of your heavenly treasure. The promises of God to you in the hope realm become reality when you act by faith. Faith requires action.

Satan will throw up barriers every time you begin to act in faith to claim the promises God has for your life. Expect trouble if you are a man or woman of faith. Problems surround anyone who believes God's promises and moves by faith to realize Kingdom reality "on earth as it is in heaven." Action to claim God's promises to you makes you an immediate target of satanic warfare.

People who lose hope have been robbed by the devil from reaching their full potential. Satan will always steal promises that God has given to you, leaving you feeling hopeless and afraid. You become immobilized to act in faith. You feel like a failure while God is saying, "Press on! You can do it! I'll make a way through this test for you."

The devil will do anything necessary to destroy your confidence as a man or woman of God. He will expose your weaknesses and condemn you with them. He will beat you over the head with your inadequacies. He will threaten you with failure as he takes advantage of your weak moments to grab the seeds of God's promises right out of your heart.

If possible, the devil will make you doubt the validity of your covenant with God. Those commitments you've made in setting priorities—seeking first the Kingdom of God—gradually lose their importance. Suddenly, people lose their perspective on God's will for them, and the next thing you know, their families are falling apart. The devil will strip you of every good gift God has placed into your hands if he can—if you allow him to.

While you are being robbed, the devil will prosper people who are unscrupulous and greedy. This discrepancy is part of the devil's strategy to torment God's people and make them doubt their covenant with the Lord. Greedy people will get rich for a season, but remember, they are like trees without deep roots. They fall suddenly with a mighty thud in the storms of life.

The devil will stir up lust to drive people into inordinate relationships that will destroy them and others. Satan can beautify those who live for vanity to get those setting spiritual direction off track. The devil has the ability to beautify evil so that a woman with the spirit of Jezebel is so beautiful she can control a king. Lust of the flesh, lust of the eyes and the pride of life become the motivation for all kinds of decisions and direction that will eventually bring destruction.

The devil has both the ability and the authority to enter into agreements with men. He can cause business deals to develop out of the blue if someone will make a deal with him. He can put you in the right place at the right time if you are useful to his scheme against God's will. This is the reason that sometimes people will give their lives to God, and all at once everything seems to fall apart. The devil has taken his hands off their lives, and he wants revenge. That revenge means reclaiming the tools he gave them to serve him.

Satan enters man through his free will, just as God does. A sovereign God has ordered that the only way for the spirit realm to enter into the flesh is through a person's freedom of choice. A person can choose to live as a temple of Satan in the same way that he can minister to others as a temple of the Holy Spirit. Either God's Holy Spirit or a spirit of darkness can indwell someone.

Just as you open the door of your heart to God to love and to serve Him, you can also open doors for Satan to invade your thoughts, your words and your actions. Satan is a type of god— with a little "g." He seeks to devour the soul of one who opens the door of his life to powers of darkness.

Satan often enters one's thoughts through emotions such as jealousy, rejection and emotional wounds caused by others— sometimes early in life. Depression is a state of mind in which people have lost their purpose and meaning. Satan robs people of their reasons for living through emotional bondage to his control. While Satan brings intellectual, emotional and spiritual death, the Spirit of the Lord brings total life. While Satan intends to destroy anything good, the joy of the Lord is your strength.

Satan plays upon natural emotions by prostituting them to some aberrated state. Normal sexual desires become perverted to homosexuality or some other means of appeasing a deviated sexual appetite. This is the reason that so many people pay mil· lions of dollars every year for pornography. Normal, wholesome passions useful for motivation and bonding between two human beings in a covenant relationship are totally aberrated. People are left living in chains to their desires—which are never satisfied.

The devil enters your thought world to redirect your decisions. Acts of worship such as fasting, praising God or giving finan· cially to the cause of God involve the decision-making pro· cesses. The devil will always attempt to interrupt meditations upon God's Word or the decision to claim the promises of God. Your thoughts are powerfully directive, and the conflicts within your mind are indisputably the most crucial area of spiritual warfare.

Don't ever underestimate the power and strength of your enemy. Don't believe the portrayals of him in some dramas that make him seem wimpy and impotent. The devil is a survivor who can take commands from God and still not give up the battle. He hears God tell him repeatedly how far he can go, yet he continually presses to the limit.

The book of Job is the classic story of God's setting limitations upon how far the devil is allowed to test someone who belongs to God. First of all, the story of Job shows that the devil is not intimidated about approaching God with a request. Many Christians are far more hesitant to approach their Father than the devil is. God grants the devil's request to destroy Job's property, then his cattle, then his children.

When Job remains true to God throughout those trials, the devil makes another proposal. The devil asks God to allow him to touch Job's body with an illness. God grants the request. Job's body is covered with sores from head to toe.

Meanwhile, the devil has sent Job three friends to comfort him. These "comforters" tell Job that everything has happened to him because he has too much pride and he has sinned. Then the devil returns and asks God if he can tamper with Job's wife's reaction to their tragedies. God grants the request, and Job's wife advises her husband to "curse God and die."

A sorrowful, confused Job remains trusting in his covenant with God. Then the devil asks, "God, can I take his life?" And notice, God says, "No! That's the limit." Job's covenant with God held secure throughout all the temptations and trials that the devil threw at him. The end of this story is the victorious restoration of all that the devil had stolen from Job.

In the story about Jesus' casting out a host of demons called "Legion," again the devil must ask permission from the Lord. These demonic spirits beg Jesus, "Sir, can we go into that herd of swine over there?" (Mark 5:9-13; Luke 8:29-34).

13

We can feel so superior to the devil in authority, yet Christians are far less respectful to God's authority than forces of darkness are. Christians seldom ask God whether they can go somewhere: what hotel they stay in, what beach they should sun on, etc. Christians think, "Those decisions are my business." Christians don't even commit themselves in agreement with God to pray about something. No wonder the Church is dead and lifeless and allowing our cities to die.

The devil knows he can be cast out. He can only oppress or possess someone who permits him to torment them. As ridiculous as it seems, some Christians want the oppression of Satan in their lives. They invite him in and entertain him as a permanent resident through some habit or practice that they refuse to give up. But when someone wants deliverance, the devil must go. He has no choice.

The devil cannot read your mind. He only reacts to your actions. Then he torments you by playing upon your weaknesses revealed through your own words and attitudes. Even then, he cannot cross the bloodline of covenant you have with God unless he gets God's permission. The devil is always limited by covenant people who have repented, honor the Sabbath, observe the Lord's table, experience baptism, tithe faithfully, and submit themselves to the counsel of spiritual elders. When the blood of the Lamb is placed over the doorpost of your life, the devil has no authority there.

OVERCOMING THE DEVIL

The Bible records three aspects of your witness that overcome the devil every time (Revelation 12:11). First, as I have stated, **you overcome by the bloodline—the blood of the Lamb.** You can never overcome the devil or his temptations without the blood of Jesus applied to your heart. You must personally know the atoning blood of Christ in your life to defeat powers of darkness.

Secondly, **you overcome the devil by your testimony.** Your testimony is your proclamation of who you are in God. You testify every time you talk about the power of God in your life. You testify whenever you do something that God has directed you to do. Your testimony is the fruit of your life—positive or negative. When your testimony lifts up Jesus and honors Him, the devil is defeated.

Finally, **the devil is defeated whenever you live as a sacrifice before God.** Sometimes that commitment may even lead to physical death. A living sacrifice trusts God with whatever will bring glory and honor to the work of His Kingdom.

A young police officer in his late twenties, Wade Barrett, Jr., a faithful member of our church, was killed as he walked into a drug raid at a local apartment complex. Wade was wearing a bullet-proof vest and was killed by the bullet of only a .25-caliber pistol. Why?

That bullet found its way through a narrow seam where the vest was joined. It pierced directly into Wade's heart. His death, though tragic and in many ways seemingly senseless in natural understanding, was not in vain. The death of this young officer happened only one week after a video of police brutality in Los Angeles made national news. The mood of the public clearly focused on the misuse of police authority. Perhaps God needed a living sacrifice to show the other side of law enforcement— caring and sacrificial.

Somehow God used Wade's death to speak to our community about responsibility and sacrifice. More than 1,800 police officers filed into our church for that funeral. All of the DeKalb County commissioners and police executives of our county were present. All three national television affiliates in Atlanta, numerous radio stations, *The Atlanta Journal and Constitution*, and other members of the press broadcast the funeral with headline coverage.

At a time when Sunday after Sunday God had told me to preach about our responsibility in addressing the conditions of our city, God used the death of this highly-respected young man to speak to hundreds of those who represent law and order on the streets every day. Only God can orchestrate the strange way He accomplishes His purposes. I charged those officers that they would work either as a shepherd over our community or as a hireling. I could not speak for them, but I knew Wade Barrett, Jr. I had seen him praying at our early morning prayer meetings. I heard young men tell me about his involvement in our youth sports programs. Wade was the kind of young man who wanted his life—and his death—to count for something!

A living sacrifice will defeat the devil even if the circumstances are confusing or difficult when they occur. Being a living sacrifice means living in an eternal dimension instead of living for the things this world can give. Being a living sacrifice means saying, "God, my life is in Your hands. Whatever You want to take place for the sake of the Kingdom of God is fine with me."

DESTROYING HIS WORKS

The devil is overcome whenever and wherever you destroy his

works. You destroy the works of the devil by standing firm against any signs of rebellion challenging what is right and good. That means correcting and protecting children you see hanging out on the streets after dark. That means doing everything you can to preserve a marriage that appears to be crumbling. Whenever something harmful or evil occurs, you must be willing to get involved and address the problems directly.

People will respond to your honest love for them. People know when you are motivated by love instead of merely gossiping or meddling in their private affairs. The devil is defeated whenever God's people reach out to those who are in trouble. We need to act in love and walk in light to destroy the works of the devil.

You defeat the devil by making no place for him in your own mind and heart. Avoid people and places that lure you into danger. The devil will place people in your life to pull you down so that he can defeat you. He knows exactly the kind of person who can be used as a snare for you. How? He studies your weaknesses.

You defeat the devil by the meditations of your heart. Often the nature of those meditations comes through your mouth in the words you speak. The devil cannot deceive someone who focuses upon God's Word at night and sings and declares a positive testimony of praise to the Lord in the morning.

You defeat the devil by staying under God's rod and staff. The Good Shepherd looks out for your well-being. Just as Christ is the Chief Shepherd, God has called men and women with the hearts of shepherds to serve and protect you in this world. People who attempt to defeat Satan in their lives without the provisions God has given them through spiritual leaders are not utilizing God's resources for their lives.

What are you doing to defeat the devil? How are you living your life?

> *Therefore you are inexcusable, O man, whoever you are who judge, for in whatever you judge another you condemn yourself; for you who judge practice the same things. But we know that the judgment of God is according to truth against those who practice such things. And do you think this, O man, you who judge those practicing such things, and doing the same, that you will escape the judgment of God? Or do you despise the riches of His goodness, forbearance, and longsuffering, not knowing that the goodness of God leads you to repentance? But in accordance with your hardness and your impenitent heart you are treasuring up for yourself wrath in the day of wrath and revelation of the righteous judgment of God, who will render to each one according to his deeds.* (Romans 2:1-6)

The rewards of God come to those who persevere with patience, continuance and determination to do good. No adherence to righteousness is ever overlooked by God. He will provide a way of escape through temptations, and He will preserve His cause through any test. Someone who knows the dimensions of spiritual warfare has no excuses before God in the day of judgment.

God's Word urges us to enter His presence with boldness (Hebrews 10:19; 4:16). Our boldness is in God and in His truth (1 Thessalonians 2:2). You enter into His presence with boldness because you are secure in His covenant, your deeds, your thoughts and your meditations.

Your boldness is equal to your love (1 John 4:17). Bold love always gets results for God, and the devil will tremble whenever someone motivated by love opens his or her mouth! He will do anything to stop that kind of bold love. Bold love was the power of Jesus' ministry. Bold love is the ministry of the glorious Church that will turn cities upside down in this hour.

Seven Steps to Victory Over the Devil

1. **Enter the hope realm and find your promise from God.** God's Word is filled with promises to you. Ask God to help you remember specific promises that He has made in your life that have been buried under disappointment and doubt. Satan has robbed you of those promises, but God desires to restore to you anything that the devil has taken. Enter boldly into your Father's presence and make your request known.

2. **Claim that promise.** You must begin declaring that you will receive whatever God has promised to you. Your faith will grow. You will begin to act upon that promise. You will decide to move in the direction of God's promises to you, and your thoughts and actions will confirm that direction.

3. **Pray.** Prayer and declaration go hand in hand to realize God's promises in your life. Prayer will keep you on track. Receiving God's promises is a process that involves moment by moment interaction with Him. He will guide and direct you as you grow in faith, and He will lead you where the lessons are that you need to know. Pray without wavering in knowing that

God is in complete control—even in control of your enemy.

4. **Believe.** Doubt will always rob you of God's promises to you. Jesus said, "When you pray, believe . . ." It seems strange that someone would pray without believing, but people do it all the time. You will live out your beliefs. Your actions will correspond with what you believe. Don't doubt. God rewards those who diligently seek Him—which means your beliefs and actions produce results.

5. **Give glory to God.** Constantly give glory to God even in the midst of tribulation. The Apostle Paul said, "In all things give thanks . . ." I preached this message to the congregation at our church in Atlanta as my mother lay dying. I declared to them the joy I felt in Christ. My confidence in facing my mother's death was centered in God's abiding presence and peace.

Remember who God is. Remember that He will never leave you nor forsake you—no matter what! When you settle that issue, nothing the enemy can do will rob you of joy. In His joy is supernatural strength to endure any test with confidence.

6. **Pay your vows to God.** In other words, keep your covenant promises to God. God will not be mocked. If you are in covenant with Him, you must abide by those agreements or face the penalty. Vows before God are serious matters that have eternal repercussions. Unless you are willing to pay your vows—even to your own hurt—God cannot protect you from evil.

7. **Remember your source.** Your source of strength is not in financial securities or education or talent. God is your source. God promises to supply your needs according to His riches in glory. That means that your needs will be met when you maintain covenant with God. Do not allow the devil to divert you to depend on anything except Him.

Our cities breed impending devastation. The challenges we face have never been greater, but the opportunities have never been more accessible to God's people. Where are the bold Christian leaders? Educators, scientists, politicians, journalists—all are waiting for people with genuine answers to step forward.

We are engaged in a mighty battle for the minds and hearts of people around the world to know hope and solutions. The blind are beginning to see. But at the same time, we must also see the enemy. And when Jesus has touched your eyes a second time to give you clear vision, you are ready to march forward and make a difference.

2 THE PROBLEM

D o you ever glance at the headlines in a newspaper and
wonder if the whole world is going to hell? Guess what?
As life on this planet edges closer toward total devastation, God
has master-minded a plan. I know it isn't obvious, but think
about it! Sometimes things get pretty rough before the answer,
the solution or the resolution to a problem becomes apparent.

For example, on January 16, 1991, the United Nations allied
forces, led by the United States, began air attacks over Iraq.
Rumors circulated that Iraqi ground soldiers were excellent
fighters with years of experience, and the effort to liberate
Kuwait from Iraqi invaders could easily become an international blood bath.

Millions of people stayed glued to television newscasts for several weeks to learn some very important lessons about winning a war. What we discovered was that training, discipline, understanding the problem and executing the procedures for a solution are the keys to winning decisive battles.

We witnessed excellent coordination between President George Bush and other coalition leaders. The military mobilization led by the Secretary of Defense and the Joint Chiefs of Staff was an example of precision state-of-the-art warfare. Our military forces emerged as national heroes.

In interviews broadcast to a "do your own thing," "I did it my way" society, we heard men and women say repeatedly, "I'm just here to do my job well to serve my country." These heroes had somehow discovered a secret of success—the value of excellent training, following orders, joining forces and working together to accomplish a common goal.

What a lesson! No wonder despair at the national debt and rising unemployment took a back seat to a euphoric surge of flag-waving patriotism. Everyone felt proud! If only the story could end there. If only we could just add the words, "lived happily ever after," and sweep the rest of history under the carpet. If only life were that simple!

——— BEING AWARE OF THE PROBLEMS ———

Every human being alive has problems. Some of the problems you face are common to all people. You need food, clothing and a home. You face physical maladies: sickness, accidents, the normal cycle of the aging process. You relate to other people which creates innumerable possibilities as well as risks to your happiness and security.

Some problems are custom-made for your particular situation. Your location can create problems for you. Your health or physical characteristics may present problems. You may have financial worries. You may have emotional problems from childhood experiences or intellectual limitations in certain areas of study. Family relationships or other relationships may present problems that are unique to your life situation.

The point is that everyone you meet has problems both like yours and unlike yours. Examining our world confirms that we live in what the Bible calls "perilous times." From birth we are thrust into a problem-laden system that can swallow us whole. What are the characteristics of perilous times?

> *. . . men will be lovers of themselves, lovers of money, boasters, proud, blasphemers, disobedient to parents, unthankful, unholy, unloving, unforgiving, slanderers, without self-control, brutal, despisers of good, traitors, headstrong, haughty, lovers of pleasure rather than lovers of God, having a form of godliness but denying its power.* (2 Timothy 3:1-5)

This list may seem personal and non-threatening individually, but because these attitudes so overwhelmingly dominate life on a global scale, world systems totter in a state of collapse. Indeed, the times are perilous. Unforgiving people unite to create an unforgiving society. Brutal people create a brutal nation. When individuals who "despise good" get together, they create a gang mentality that terrorizes an entire city.

People with a "form of godliness without the power" of the Holy Spirit create dead churches. This "form of godliness" cannot set people free from their bondages of sin. So what happens? People on drugs never even consider the church as a place of deliverance. People getting a divorce talk to a bartender instead of a pastor. Suicide seems like the best alternative to a dilemma in life.

Depressed enough yet? Yes, problems abound. The systems of this world are collapsing, but the solution is also beginning to emerge simultaneously. The Bible puts it this way: "And the world is passing away, and the lust of it; but he who does the will of God abides forever."

". . . He who does the will of God" can be both individual and collective. A man or woman who does God's will is a mighty witness with great influence, but a group of people who are dedicated to doing God's will can turn their community around.

Here's the shocking news: This is the day of the local church! Now hear me out! The time has come for God to demonstrate His glory around the world through people like you and me who know Him, love the truth and are willing to do whatever He asks.

You're thinking, "Bishop Paulk, you've got to be kidding! Most of the churches I've visited are dead, dead, dead!" All I can say is you better get ready for a wonderful surprise! In the midst of the greatest problems that any generation in history has ever faced, the local church is coming alive with the solutions!

SOME NEW BATTLEFIELDS

These perilous times have taken their toll upon the thought processes of Christians and non-Christians alike. Compromises in truth and righteous standards have blurred the lines distinguishing good and evil. The first battle the local church must address is bringing its concept of life's purpose into total accord with God's perspective. What are these battlefields?

PROBLEM ONE: The loss of the concept of sin.

Until you know the true definition of sin, how can you ever know the joy that follows confession and repentance before God? Sin has become a toy for the classroom—a subject for discussion and debate. Psychologists and sociologists have softened the concept of sin with words like "dysfunctional," "co-dependent" and "narcissistic."

What is sin? What stirs the anger of God? Jesus drove money-changers out of the temple because they were offering people false hope. He railed against Pharisees who walked around like they had all the answers when they not only didn't know God themselves, but also made knowing God more difficult for the people. Jesus reprimanded His disciples for wanting to call down fire from heaven to punish people disagreeing with them. He cursed a tree that didn't produce fruit. He chided His disciples for their lack of faith.

Often Christians spend their time crusading to clean up sins that God would bypass to zero in on the heart issues causing that sin. Lust causes adultery. Hatred causes murder. Drug addictions are often caused by hopelessness and the need for an escape from harsh realities.

We know more about the consequences of sin than we do about the definition of sin. We hack away at the branches instead of laying an axe to the root problem. We debate the issues of abortion, divorce and AIDS without pinpointing the root problem of "sin" in someone's life—and the need for repentance—the only road leading to true healing. Only the blood of Jesus Christ can cleanse us of our sins.

PROBLEM TWO: The lack of demonstration of standards today.

Who sets the standards in our society today? Madonna? Michael Jackson? Cher? Mike Tyson? Michael Jordan? Who are the role models? What influence forms the values that your children accept as standards for their lives? Television soap operas? Violent "R"-rated movies? Situation comedies? Models in fashion magazines?

Moses cried out to God that people didn't even comprehend what He meant by moral behavior, so God called Moses to the mountain and gave him the law. The Ten Commandments provided mankind with a conscience about what is acceptable and unacceptable behavior. A person's conscience is trained. An improperly trained conscience may instigate unjustified guilt in a child. But God's Law provides us with clear definitions of sin. Without having a clear understanding of standards, we cannot understand sin.

Without clear standards of goodness and truth, an entire society has no conscience. Anything goes. If it feels good, do it! No one is accountable for his actions. No one is responsible for the pain he causes in someone else's life. It's every man for himself—every woman for herself!

What has happened to the standards set in the home, the school and the church? Family values are regarded as old-fashioned in America today. Today the normal family is a married couple—one of whom has been divorced—and one child in daycare. Home has become merely a check-point station. Meals are eaten on the run. People living in the same house never see or talk with one another.

School has become a danger zone for drugs, violence and sexual information. Educational standards have fallen so drastically that standardized tests have to be adjusted for lower reading levels. Illiteracy is growing in spite of our media-obsessed society. American education lags far behind educational standards of other high-tech nations.

And where are the standards in the local church? If a man can preach, he hits the road with his traveling seminar. If someone can sing well, she looks for an agent to make her a gospel music star. Excellence in any area of ministry translates into "take this to the world and make some money!" Meanwhile the local church sets standards in mediocrity and getting by. Members send monthly support to their favorite televangelist and tip God as the offering plate passes by on Sundays.

Jesus set standards in love and compassion that countered the religious system of His day. He said, "You have heard of old . . . but I say to you . . ." His standards opened wide the Kingdom of God to the poor, the needy, the hungry, the sick and the dying. He lifted the woman taken in adultery from the dust and ate dinner at the home of a crooked tax collector.

PROBLEM THREE: Misuse of the Word of God.

The Bible has become nothing more than a proof text to

substantiate our doctrines and theories. I find it helpful to differentiate between "the Bible" and the "Word of God." Of course the Bible is the Word of God, but we often use it for more than to hear God's voice.

We use the Bible to prove our points. We try to make Scripture fit our ideas about the end of the age and the coming of Christ. Some scriptures are used repeatedly, while other passages that don't fit our ideas are totally ignored.

If I were not a Christian, I would have difficulty believing that the Church could tell me anything about the outcome of world events. Prophets have proclaimed so much error—the date of the rapture, Armageddon in the war with Iraq, the identity of the Antichrist (because of a birthmark on Gorbachev's head). The world laughs at these self-proclaimed prophets, and the church loses its credibility.

The person of Jesus is lost in our academic discussions about Him. We analyze His words as philosophical text instead of allowing the Lord to instruct us. We read the footnotes instead of what the Bible is saying. We know about Jesus Christ instead of knowing Him. John wrote about the Bible:

> *". . . but these are written that you may believe that Jesus is the Christ, the Son of God, and that believing you may have life in His name."* (John 20:31)

Properly using the Word of God always brings life. God's Word always lifts up Jesus and points you in the direction of abundant living. The Holy Spirit brings God's Word alive for those who are seeking God's direction.

> *For the Word of God is living and powerful, and sharper than any two-edged sword, piercing even to*

the division of soul and spirit, and of joints and mar-
row, and is a discerner of the thoughts and intents of
the heart. (Hebrews 4:12)

Is this your experience with the Word of God? If not, why?
The Bible has been improperly used in the Church for everything except as a life-changing revelation of Jesus Christ.

PROBLEM FOUR: Confusion between the Church and the Kingdom.

After teaching about the Kingdom of God for some years
now, I've become increasingly aware of confusion between distinguishing the Church from the Kingdom of God. The Church
on earth is not the Kingdom of God.

What is the Kingdom of God? The Kingdom of God is the
totality of created beings, spirits and powers, who at any given
time are submitted to the Lordship of Jesus Christ.

So what is the Church? The Church is the redeemed of all
times, both the redeemed in heaven and the redeemed on
earth, and those to be saved in the future before the coming of
the Lord.

The redeemed of the Church include both Old Testament
and New Testament saints along with Christians through the
centuries. The Apostle Paul refers to the Church in heaven and
on earth. The Church is the home for God's family. The
Church is the seat of government for God's work here on earth.
Through the Church, God reaches out to a lost world in darkness with hope and light.

The Bible never instructs Christians to preach "the Church."
We are instructed to proclaim "the Kingdom of God." I dis-
courage people at Chapel Hill Harvester Church from promot-

ing their church in place of the gospel of the Kingdom. Of course I'm delighted that members love our fellowship and invite others to come, but the message to change that non-believer is the gospel.

Jesus told Nicodemas, "You must be born again to enter the kingdom of God." Did He teach about Church membership? No! Jesus told the Pharisee about the Kingdom (John 3).

Jesus sent out His disciples on an evangelistic tour. He told them, "As you go, preach to people, saying, 'The kingdom of heaven is at hand.'" Have you ever wondered why Jesus didn't instruct those disciples to give information on the synagogues in their neighborhoods? Jesus simply told them to preach the Kingdom and then heal the sick, cleanse the lepers, raise the dead and cast out devils. He said, "Freely you have received, freely give" (Matthew 10:7-8).

One of the most outstanding evangelists in the New Testament was Philip. The Book of Acts records Philip's dynamic ministry by saying, "But when they believed Philip as he preached the things concerning the kingdom of God . . ." (Acts 8:12). Why didn't Philip preach on the Church? Only the gospel of the Kingdom changed lives and turned the world upside down.

Jesus called the disciples to preach the kingdom of God. Jesus, Himself, preached the Kingdom of God from city to city, and He was moved with compassion when He saw that people were scattered like sheep having no shepherd. He didn't organize a church for them! He preached the Kingdom of God, and the church grew out of that revelation of His Kingdom.

So what is the point? When one preaches the Church itself, those listening hear the words of a self-serving, self-sustaining organization speaking in its own behalf. When one preaches the Kingdom of God, the Church is built!

Jesus Christ was the incarnation of the Kingdom of God. In Jesus, in the incarnation, the Kingdom of God had a name and a face. Up until the birth of Christ, the Kingdom had been represented by the Ark of the Covenant. Throughout the history of Israel, God had been present with His people to effect change in the fallen world order. The Kingdom of God that is spiritual must be so comprehended and applied as salt and light that it affects the community in which it exists. When the Kingdom of God comes, circumstances change drastically!

The Church may not affect any circumstances surrounding you, but the Kingdom always changes things. Churches that preach and demonstrate Kingdom authority will grow. For example, I had a visit recently from the head of the department of evangelism of a Presbyterian seminary in our area. He looked me right in the eyes and said, "Bishop Paulk, we have six churches within a few miles of your church that are dying, and you are adding almost two thousand members a year. Can you give me some insight on why this is happening?"

I answered, "It's the power of the gospel of the Kingdom that awakens the potential in people who are seeking God. People want to know how to become a part of the Kingdom of God and how to apply its principles in everyday living to change the world for good."

A WARNING

Now I must warn you that the message can take two

extremes that will defeat God's purposes. One extreme causes people to totally internalize and spiritualize Kingdom principles so that they go down a trail of pietism and Pharisaism that leads to pacifism. To regard the Kingdom of God as nothing more than a spiritual realm that never touches the earth will totally destroy the power and effectiveness of the message.

The other extreme leads people to a religious organization. That activism can promote a "take-over" mentality that is not the same as a witness of the Kingdom. Unrestrained zeal to enforce a Kingdom demonstration can create a political revolution that does not represent the character of Christ at all. Polarization of Kingdom goals can lead to some very dangerous conclusions.

So an internalized interpretation of the gospel of the Kingdom has no impact on earth, while an external interpretation of the Kingdom becomes a radical political movement. Neither of these extremes bear the fruit that Jesus taught us exemplifies the fruit of His Spirit.

So How Does the Kingdom Work?

Let me follow warnings with a positive statement. The proper working of the Kingdom requires that we build our lives upon the foundation of God's Word which blends His law with His love and grace so as to bring about change in society. God's Word provides an unshakeable foundation. God's law trains your conscience toward pleasing God. God's love and grace draw those seeking answers to Christ. When these factors are working properly, a community, a city or a nation is changed.

The Old Testament teaches certain expectations of the Kingdom of God.

1. **The Kingdom of God brings the presence and the glory of God to Israel.** This presence is represented by the Ark of the Covenant in the Old Testament. Israel served as God's representative people. Though the dimension of Israel's representation of God to the world has changed, some people still cling to this Old Testament concept of God's presence and glory.

2. **The Kingdom of God will overcome the powers of darkness.** God promises an overcoming power throughout the Bible to crush the serpent, beginning with the story of the Garden of Eden (Genesis 3:15). The crushing of Satan's head is a theme throughout Scripture as a promise to the redeemed of their final victory through Christ.

3. **The Kingdom of God will provide salvation for sin.** Throughout the Old Testament, God promised Israel a new heart, a cleansing for sin through mercy and forgiveness. Though many Old Testament concepts emphasized God's judgment, they were also promised God's grace upon them.

4. **The Kingdom of God would reach from the nation of Israel to encompass people of the entire earth.** The Old Testament books of Isaiah and Micah were especially insistent that God's Kingdom would reach people to the north, south, east and west. Micah extended pleasing God beyond obedience to the Law by declaring that God required people to love justice and mercy and walk humbly before Him. The Old Testament is filled with references to a transcendent covenant beyond the people of Israel.

New Testament expectations of the Kingdom of God included all the things promised in the Old Testament, but the commission of Christ to His Church adds the importance of world influence in the other things we are to expect.

1. **The Kingdom of God will impact the world through the Church's influence as "salt" and "light."** Jesus' first sermon set the agenda for the Church. He preached that His anointing from God empowered Him to preach the gospel to the poor, to heal the brokenhearted, to set captives free, to give sight to the blind, to deliver those who are oppressed and to proclaim the acceptable year of the Lord (Luke 4:18,19).

John needed to be convinced that Jesus was the Messiah as he sat in prison awaiting his execution. Jesus sent word to John that the blind were seeing, the lame were walking—all the evidence of Kingdom power in His ministry (Matthew 11:4-12). The evidence of the Kingdom of God at work is power that impacts lives.

2. **The Kingdom of God from Jesus' perspective was both present and future.** Jesus said that the Kingdom of God is "at hand," meaning in the present. You receive the Kingdom of God now, but you enter into it hereafter (Mark 1:14,15). The concept of the present and future Kingdom has been one of the most misunderstood principles of Kingdom teaching in this present move of God.

3. **The Kingdom of God is ultimate, absolute, eternal and infinite.** Notice, I do not attribute those same definitions to the Church. We are presently on assignment in preparing for the full manifestation of the Kingdom of God. In this hour, we war against the gates of hell. We wrestle against powers and princi-palities in heavenly conflict. We witness daily to the power and presence of God at work in the world.

KINGDOM PRECEPTS

No one can ever hope to see or to enter the Kingdom of God without understanding certain foundational truths.

1. **The Kingdom of God is visible only to people of faith.** Jesus explained this by comparing the effects of the Kingdom of God to watching the wind blow (John 3:8). You easily recognize the effects of the wind blowing, but you do not see the wind.

So how do you recognize a church teaching the Kingdom of God? Seeing a church with people sitting inside does not necessarily make them participants in the work of the Kingdom of God. You cannot separate the work of the Kingdom from the work of the Holy Spirit. If you separate the power of Pentecost from the Kingdom, you will never understand God's purposes for His Church.

I traveled to Baton Rouge four or five years ago and stood for several hours before Bible scholars from a well-known ministry in that city. They had challenged me on the teaching of the Kingdom of God. I answered their questions for four hours, and finally I said to that group of people with old line Pentecostal theology, "I just want you to answer one question for me. Why was the Holy Ghost given?"

The room was totally silent. They taught that Jesus was coming any minute to snatch us out of all our problems. Many Pentecostals have believed that the Holy Spirit was given to make them shout, holler and scream. No one wanted to admit that Pentecostal power equips us as witnesses and overcomers against world systems in daily living.

The disciples asked Jesus at His Ascension if He would now restore the Kingdom to Israel, thinking of a political rule for their nation. Jesus must have thought, "I've taught you all this time, and you still don't understand . . ." Jesus then told them to go to Jerusalem where they would be endued with power. Power for what? It's time that the Church understands the answer to that question.

2. **The Church is the instrument of the Kingdom ideal.** The Church is the means of Kingdom expression—a visible expression of God's Kingdom. Do we fail at that? Oh, yes! But God has not given up on us yet! Even though we are always an imperfect representation of the perfection of biblical truth, we are used by God to impart His truth and grace.

That precept explains why some churches grow and others are dying. Some churches will not allow certain people in their doors. They do not want homosexuals or AIDS patients or divorced people to sit among them. Jesus stands at the door saying, "Come, come, come!" while members of the Church are saying, "Go, go, go! We don't want your problems!"

In Atlanta we are building a Cathedral to the Holy Spirit with a spire that reaches to the sky. That spire says to anyone in our community that God is present among them. They are welcome in their Father's house! Our congregation is certainly not perfect, but we've touched the Kingdom reality that is, and we can share that reality with others. We compel people into our church—all are needed and wanted!

3. **The Kingdom is seated in the heart and the will of the believer.** In this regard, the Kingdom of God is a mystery. The Church, on the other hand, is no mystery, but the Kingdom of God within the Church is. For example, how is it that elders

praying over crack babies are able to see them healed? Miracles happen every day by praying over a situation.

The Kingdom of God within us is inexhaustible and unshakeable. Meanwhile, world systems are collapsing. The Kingdom of God offers the only solution in a time of devastation, and Jesus said to preach it, teach it and demonstrate it so that He could judge the systems of this world by it.

Stephen, as he was stoned by a mob, looked up to heaven and saw Jesus standing at the right hand of the Father. Stephen understood that the power of the Kingdom of God transcended life. Do you ever consider what life is like after we die? Streets of gold? Sitting with your feet dangling in a brook? Holding hands with someone special for a billion years? Frankly, none of these scenes appeal to me personally, but I know I'll enjoy God's eternal presence.

The very fact that we can comprehend life after death means that it exists. Pigs, dogs and squirrels don't care what happens after they die, but people—saved or unsaved—do care! One day the Church will have served its purpose, but the Kingdom of God is from everlasting to everlasting.

4. **The proclamation of the Kingdom of God produces revolution and change.** I'm sure the word "revolution" is too strong for some people, so just think "change." Change what? The lives of people in public housing by teaching them to read. The lives of AIDS patients by sharing Christ's love for them. Anywhere the works of the devil appear, we are there to turn the situation around to bring glory to God's Kingdom.

First comes the proclamation, then change follows. We have another King besides President Bush or Premier Gorbachev. There is another King (Acts 17:7,8). The proclamation of His

Kingdom changes families, cities and nations as human hearts receive their King.

5. **When the Kingdom of God is received by faith, people begin to recognize its distinctives, respond to its demands and receive its blessings, rewards and protection.** Recognizing the distinctives of the Kingdom of God is the result of the Holy Spirit, our Teacher and Guide, within us. He makes us sensitive to discern truth and error.

People begin to respond to the demands of the Kingdom of God because the inner, compelling force of the Holy Spirit presses them toward a bold witness. All personal decisions are made on the basis of how that decision will impact your witness. You want to know God's Word. You want to share fellowship with people who know and love the Lord as you do. You want to tithe into the work of the Lord.

People who really understand the Kingdom of God not only tithe, but they also plant seeds of faith for a harvest. They give to God's cause out of their own needs—personal, financial, physical, spiritual—so that God can bless them in abundance. I don't focus on a "prosperity" message, per se, but I am absolutely certain that God prospers people who exercise this precept of giving when they have a need to be met.

God's covenants are fulfilled in secret places. In covenant, God makes a way of escape from attacks of the devil on your life. While other people are falling apart right and left, you'll have a solution. Under the Lordship of Christ, you'll have protection. That doesn't mean you won't have problems every day, but God will not allow you to be overtaken by any strategy of darkness waged against you to destroy you. Your covenant with God is foolproof!

Now that we've explored the problems, I will share what people like you and I are supposed to do about the problems. We have a tremendous challenge in the days ahead leading toward the 21st Century. You, personally, have exciting things to look forward to! Never allow the problems to overwhelm you—God has a plan! And you are part of His plan!

Jesus saw the problems in Jerusalem. He wept, "Oh, Jerusalem, Jerusalem! How often I would have taken you . . ." I'm sure Jesus looked over that city and knew that He could have saved it from devastation. He could hear the drumbeats of destruction coming upon that city in 70 A.D. He heard the cries of children as they were slaughtered. But Jerusalem rejected the voice of God.

With prophetic insight I declare that the time has come again that the Spirit of the Lord is crying out over our cities. There is a solution, a way out. If we don't listen to God, revolution and bloodshed will flow in our streets. Buildings will lie in shambles. Leaders will not be found to give any direction, because it's already too late.

The greatest conflict in the next fifty years will erupt between the "haves" and the "have nots." The middle class is rapidly disappearing, and revolution always follows economic upheaval. The only solution is found in the Kingdom of God and the rule of Jesus Christ.

In that spirit, I cry out, "Oh, Atlanta, Detroit, New York, Dallas, Seattle, Los Angeles, Moscow, London, Cape Town . . . Hear the Word of the Lord before it's too late!"

Jesus says to you, standing before Him in judgment, "I was hungry, and you didn't feed Me. I was naked, and you didn't clothe Me . . . Your insensitivity stirred up bitterness, rejection and anger in those needing the hope I gave to you that you buried. Now they cannot be restrained."

The problems are great indeed! Anger becomes violence which becomes wars and rumors of wars. But those are only the birth pangs of the culmination of all the ages. Until that final moment, many will walk in Armageddon, that valley of decision. Antichrists will deceive many by saying that Christ has not come to earth as a man who impacted His circumstances with Kingdom authority. Many will say that the Church is totally irrelevant, powerless and out-dated.

But just wait! Watch! Pray! Then, do whatever He tells you to do. When the gospel of the Kingdom has been demonstrated as a witness around the world, then the end will come (Matthew 24:14). World systems will be judged! And Jesus Christ will reign as all in all!

3 THE PEOPLE

Every problem in the world began with the rebellion of Lucifer. Rebellion against God is the bottom line of all the chaos and devastation you see around you today. You may feel as if your particular battles have nothing to do with Lucifer's fall, but you are mistaken. Every problem and conflict on this planet is connected with totally restoring the rule of all creation to God.

The entire Bible can be summarized as God's plan for bringing the universe under God's dominion. All rebellion will end one day. And the obedience of God's people cannot be omitted as the necessary ingredient in hastening that day—the coming of the Lord.

So in addressing the subject of God's people, I must remind you again that the Church and the Kingdom are not the same. Allow me to say again, "The Kingdom is anything that God created: any people, any being, any power that is subjected to God." The Church is merely redeemed people who reflect the Kingdom of God.

What is the message of God's people? The early church taught the rule of Christ in His eternal Kingdom. Listen to the words of Jews alarmed at the message:

> *"They who have turned the world upside down have come here too. Jason has harbored them, and these are all acting contrary to the decrees of Caesar, say-ing there is another king—Jesus." And they troubled the crowd and the rulers of the city when they heard these things. So when they had taken security from Jason and the rest, they let them go. Then the brethren immediately sent Paul and Silas away by night to Berea. When they arrived, they went into the synagogue of the Jews. They were more fair-minded than those in Thessalonica, in that they received the word with all readiness and searched the scriptures daily to find out whether these things were so. There-fore, many of them believed; and also not a few of the Greeks, prominent women as well as men.* (Acts 17:6-12)

These people (fired-up Christians) were acting contrary to the decrees of Caesar or worldly governments by proclaiming another King and another kingdom. When God's people declare His rulership, worldly governments always feel threatened and assume you are making a political challenge to their authority. Though the meek will inherit the earth, God's Word calls His people "special, royal and chosen." We are "light" living in a world of darkness.

God's people transcend any ethnic, cultural or racial delineation around the world. God's Word calls us "a people who were not a people" (1 Peter 2:10). What does that mean? Christians from every tribe, language, nation or region who live or have lived in obedience to God throughout history are spiritually joined together as one holy nation. We are not characterized as being black or white, Jew or Gentile, Arab or Greek, rich or poor, but we all march daily under the banner of Christ.

Have you ever thought that these are the same people for whom Jesus felt such compassion that He called them "sheep without a shepherd"? Once we were scattered around the globe, totally unrelated and divided from one another. Now we are one nation through hearing and obeying God's voice. God always has His chosen people somewhere who hear and obey Him.

God's people do not necessarily include all the ones sitting in churches on Sunday mornings. How many people really go to worship God and receive teaching from His Word? Many people are members of a church out of habit, family ties or social associations. These don't have the slightest idea what the Spirit of God desires for their lives.

God's chosen people walk to another drumbeat. They don't live to please themselves or for the charms this world offers them. The chosen generation lives for rewards that transcend this life. They choose the rewards of God's Kingdom by their own free will.

God took the risk of His creation's rebellion by granting free will. Without free will, there could be no rebellion. First Lucifer rebelled, and then he persuaded one third of the heavenly host to follow after him. But God, though challenged in a heavenly realm by His own creation, has a solution to end rebellion.

God's Plan to End Rebellion

God created another form of life in His own image. This life form was also granted free will, the power to make the right choices or the wrong choices. Throughout history that plan of God has never changed. Amazingly, the plan of God rests upon God's belief that man will make the right choices. The Bible says that all of creation "stands on tiptoe" to see God's people come into the fullness of His promise of full restoration (Romans 8:22-25).

God placed His created beings, Adam and Eve, in an environment of absolute perfection. Together in agreement this man and woman formed the likeness of God. The joining of a man and woman in agreement before God is one of the highest revelations of God's identity that exists. That is the reason that the family unit and family values are under such attack from every direction in modern society.

God told this man and woman that they had the right of free choice. Their choices were simplified. They would enjoy absolute freedom in God's creation except for eating from the "tree of life" and the "tree of the knowledge of good and evil." God warned them of "death" for disobedience. When they ate the fruit of those trees, His life-giving Spirit would no longer protect them.

What did eating the fruit of those trees represent? That decision indicated that the man and woman were no longer submitted to God's authority. They would be saying in essence, "I want to submit to my own ingenuity, abilities and talents, God. I don't need for You to tell me what to do. I can be a god just like You!"

Of course, the woman made the wrong choice because she was deceived. God's plan for mankind to subdue the earth was jeopardized in that critical moment. Then the man willfully made the wrong choice also. Though it appeared that Lucifer had won, the battle between God and rebellious forces in the universe filtered down to one promise that God declared in His sovereignty. He told Lucifer that out of the seed of the woman would come the standard of obedience that would finally bruise his head (Genesis 3:15).

Who is that standard of obedience? Jesus came to destroy the works of the devil. That was His purpose, and the summation of the message of the entire Bible. Where mankind had failed to carry out God's plan of restoration, Jesus Christ overcame the rebellion against God that was the bondage gripping all creation. Throughout the Bible, God speaks to men and women in this unredeemed state with the promise of eventual redemption.

RESPONDING TO GOD'S VOICE

One of the first people to hear God speaking was Noah. Noah responded to God's voice by building an ark. He probably asked, "Where do You want me to build it, God?"

God answered, "In your backyard, Noah."

"But God, there's no water there!"

"I know. You don't even know what rain is, Noah. Just do as I have told you."

So in faith and obedience, Noah carried out God's explicit instructions and opened the way for God to destroy rebellion in the earth.

After God has preserved Noah and his family through the flood, Noah ends up in a drunken state. His own son uncovers his father's nakedness. Now Noah—a man used mightily by God—lies intoxicated in a state of rebellion. What is God going to do? Give up? No, God will find other men and women who will make the right choices and give their lives to fulfilling God's plan.

God's voice booms out of heaven, "Abram, Abram . . ."

"Oh, yes, I hear You. I don't know who You are, but I hear You calling me."

"Abram, I am God."

"Who is God? There are all kinds of gods where I live in Ur."

But the voice rang true in Abram's heart, and he left all that he knew in life to follow that voice's direction. Abram's obedience again demonstrated the kind of heart that overcomes rebellion in the earth. Abram—or Abraham—became the father of the household of faith. Abraham's life story, which includes the willingness to sacrifice his son at God's command, says that rebellion can be defeated by making the right choices of your own free will.

Abraham's seed—Isaac, Jacob, the twelve sons of Jacob who represent the twelve tribes of Israel—became a nation of people trapped in Egypt. Unlike the patriarch Abraham, these people do not hear God's voice. After years go by, God touches the life of Moses. God instructs Moses to go to Egypt and lead these people—rebellious and disobedient—out of bondage. God has heard their cries for deliverance.

THE LAW, A PARENTHESIS

Moses obeys God by leading Israel into the wilderness toward the promised land. Still the people are rebellious and they complain against both God and Moses. They insist upon rules and laws because their hearts are too rebellious even to discern right from wrong. So God gives them laws. The Law served as a parenthesis between the heart-response of Abraham to God's voice, and the spiritual oneness of the Father and the Son that Jesus ministered to the world. The Law certainly didn't make rebellious people good or spiritually tune their ears to hear God. The Law only pointed out man's natural gravitation toward sin.

The Bible teaches that no man is justified before God by keeping the Law, because its standard is a perfection that is impossible for man to achieve. The Law convinces you that you are a sinner. When we begin to think someone is perfect, we just put them up against the Law and we discover quickly that "all have sinned and fallen short of the glory of God."

The parenthesis of the Law set God's standard of obedience for His people for generations. Then God spoke to Mary, a young, teenage girl. God told Mary that she would have a baby conceived by God Himself. What is the response of the "second Eve" to God's plan?

That teenage girl responds to God by saying, "So be it unto me." At that moment obedience is conceived in Mary's womb. The angelic choir sang that the Savior, the Prince of Peace, is born. In Jesus Christ, the Kingdom of God is born in the flesh. When we look at Jesus, we see, touch and know how the Kingdom of God looks, what it says and what it does.

Jesus is the Kingdom of God with a face. His words say to us, "This is what God thinks." His actions tell us, "This is what God does." Little children crowd around Him and the disciples say, "He is too busy."

But the Kingdom of God responds, "I'm not too busy to bless these children. They are important to Me." And not only those who are innocent and easy to love get His attention. He goes to a demoniac with a tormented mind living in the tombs. The Kingdom of God sets him free from agonizing spirits. He eats dinner with a corrupt tax collector. He lifts a girl caught in the act of adultery from the ground and says to her, "You were created for a greater purpose than this."

Everyone He touched felt God—God in the flesh. At last the Kingdom of God had a name, a face, an address. Jesus told His disciples to look at Him for the answers to questions they debated about what God is like. Every moment of His life was given freely in total submission to the Father's voice.

THE CHURCH IN SUBMISSION

So where does the Church get its direction? I wish so much that I could say that we are as submitted to the Father's voice as Christ was. That obedience is Jesus' instruction to us. That obedience is the purpose of the Holy Spirit within us. That obedience is the reason that you and I were born into this world. But too often, the Church operates as just another secular organization.

For the most part, what we call "the Church" today is not the Church at all. Who and where is the true Church? Jesus told the disciples, "I'm going away. You go to Jerusalem and wait until the Holy Spirit comes. Then you will be endued with power and authority to accomplish the obedience that will overcome the devil." That is the phase the true Church is experiencing presently.

It's interesting that of all the thousands that Jesus taught and fed, only 120 people met together in that upper room. Most pastors of large ministries would understand that ratio. Thousands of members come to church, hear the Word of God and go their way. Only a very small percentage sitting in church on Sunday morning are spiritually tuned to God's voice with submitted hearts.

Thousands of people go to church, clap their hands, sing happy songs, and then live their lives the way they want to. If the economy collapsed, and the air conditioner broke, and the seats were too hard, and the services lasted overtime more than fifteen minutes, the majority of the members would move on.

But God always has a remnant. Jesus said that "few" find the path leading to His Kingdom. Why? It's a path demanding obedience. That is the reason that few churches and few Christians are the least bit threatening in destroying the works of the devil.

And the universal Church is fighting itself. I don't think Christ is coming tomorrow! How can the Bridegroom possibly marry such a divided bride? It reminds me of the joke about these newlyweds on their wedding night. The bride is getting ready for bed, and she pulls off her clothes, then her wig, then her artificial eye, then her teeth, then her padded bra, then her artificial leg, then her girdle. The poor bridegroom stares in amazement and says, "I don't know what to love!"

What part of the Church would Jesus claim as His bride? Every member of the Body of Christ is at war with every other member. How can we ever come into unity of purpose and Spirit? God is looking for people of obedience—not good doctrine, not strategy, not impressive buildings. Obedience means that the sacraments of baptism and the Lord's table, tithing faithfully and observing the Sabbath are not optional for God's people.

Celebrating the sacraments brings us into harmony with other Christians. The covenants of God unite us as nothing else can. When hearts are open to God in obedience, people come into unity of mind and spirit.

I am sorry to say that many people know a false sense of security in regard to their eternal salvation. They believe that their "goodness" will pay the price. No! Sins of the flesh are dealt with through confession and repentance. Forgiveness of others and seeking forgiveness for yourself is a vital part of the covenant of God. Beyond forgiveness of our sins is living out our purpose and direction according to God's plan. This is where most people miss the mark.

Most Christians believe that they are in charge of their lives— and they are! They go to church once or twice a month, throw a tip in the offering, do a few good deeds here and there and feel certain that they are bound for heaven! Take warning! The Kingdom of God is righteousness, peace and joy in the Holy Spirit, and that only comes to people who walk in obedience to the Lord.

TRANSCENDENT, INEXHAUSTIBLE AND UNSHAKEABLE

People of obedience to God understand that the Kingdom of God is transcendent, inexhaustible and unshakeable. The transcendent Kingdom cannot be confined in any way—racially, culturally, geographically, etc. The Kingdom of God encompasses all who will hear and follow the voice of the Lord.

The inexhaustible Kingdom never runs out of energy, resources, talent, finances, creativity or opportunities. Everything that is good and true has no limit in the Kingdom of God. Churches or people may exhaust themselves, but they cannot exhaust the Kingdom. Jesus knew how to tap the resources of the Kingdom of God for food, healing, protection, finances, and the like. He knew that God's provisions were available to facilitate His will.

The unshakeable Kingdom ensures victory over every obstacle in life. Nothing given up or lost for the sake of the Kingdom is ever relinquished in vain. God is not surprised by any new developments. He has the final word over every circumstance. People can be shaken by fear, doubt or trouble, but the Kingdom of God stands firmly established for eternity.

And because the Kingdom of God is transcendent, inexhaustible and unshakeable, we labor with one objective. That unselfish objective is the rule of Christ in all human experience. That objective allows for flexibility in policy, political governments, denominational distinctives, eschatological concepts, and other areas. We may never agree on all the particular concepts of biblical interpretation. Our cultural variances may never be aligned. Nevertheless, Jesus prayed that we would be one.

Jesus said, "Father, make them one . . ." (John 17). Notice that Jesus never prayed for our doctrines to be consistent. He never emphasized that the government of our churches conform with one another. Instead He prayed for the Father to make us one so that world systems would be forced to acknowledge a standard against their rebellion. An end to rebellion is what the Kingdom of God is all about.

Unity is not the same as fellowship. You can have fellowship by singing, choirs competing or sponsoring a preaching contest. But true unity means that I respect your gift and you respect mine. We know one another by the Spirit. The Holy Spirit brings us into unity beyond merely enjoying fellowship with one another.

People in obedience to God know one another by the Spirit. You also recognize those who have their own private agendas. I meet ministers known around the world by their television ministries, and I know in my spirit that they are off track in submitting to God's purposes for their lives. I hope I don't seem to be judgmental. I simply know them by discernment, and if they ask me, I'll tell them that they are not in the place God wants them to be.

God's people are special people who have laid aside their own agendas. They have chosen God's purposes by their own free wills, and they resist Satan's attempts to divert their direction. Only a demonstration of that kind of obedience sets standards against world systems in a world running out of answers and groping for solutions.

————— ## God's Process With People —————

The Old and New Testament are valuable in giving us insights and examples of how God deals with His people. God's relationship with Adam and Eve before the fall gives us a picture of life inside the Kingdom of God. The prophet Samuel came close to establishing a theocracy among God's people, but they cried out, "Give us a king!"

God consoled Samuel by telling him, "They haven't rejected you, Samuel, they have rejected Me" (1 Samuel 8:7). From that time on, men have ruled over mankind instead of being under God's rule. Obedience to God has been a dimensional experience in life that is totally individual—rather than corporate or (much less) national.

As a result of man's insistence upon human rule over him, he has fallen into harsh judgment. Pleasing man does not equal pleasing God. In many of the prophetic books of the Old Testament—Malachi, for example—God spews out judgments against the people because they have transgressed so far from obedience to Him.

God calls into account all His people who complain about their lack of prosperity. They cry, "The evil get rich, while I get more and more poor." God begins to chasten His people. He tells them, essentially, that they have robbed Him. Why does God insist that the full tithe come into the storehouse? (Malachi 4:5,6). Does God need money? No! God needs obedient hearts that extend all the way to one's pocketbook.

The Incarnation—the revelation of the New Testament—demonstrates perfect obedience to God. Jesus felt all the temptations of manhood without sinning. Jesus perfectly overcame every diversion Satan threw in His path. Jesus released people from illnesses, distresses and religious bondages. He demonstrated that God walked among us.

Old Testament prophetic utterances became a New Testament experience for the early Church. God would no longer just raise up a prophet as one voice crying out His warnings or declarations, but the prophetic cry would sound around the world through God's people. The purpose of God's people would be the same purpose as Christ's ministry. Like Him, they would destroy the works of the devil.

The Church becomes the trustholder of promoting the rule and reign of Christ. Of course, we have a Helper that guides the strategy of our witness. The theocracy we promote is really a Christocracy in which Jesus is declared King of kings and Lord of lords in every sphere of life.

THE CHRISTOCRACY BECOMING A THEOCRACY

Our witness is based upon demonstrating Christ within us. We say to the world, "This is what Christ says; this is what Christ instructed us to do; this is Christ's response to that situation." Jesus lived as God in the flesh, and the Church bears witness to Christ, living as evidence of His Spirit at work in the world today.

The eventual reign of Christ over all creation is a fact of destiny. And that promise gives us great confidence in our labor.

> *For He must reign until He has put all enemies under His feet. The last enemy that will be destroyed is death. For "He has put all things under His feet." But when He*

says, "All things are put under Him," it is evident that He who put all things under Him is excepted. Now when all things are made subject to Him, then the Son Himself will also be subject to Him who put all things under Him, that God may be all in all. (1 Corinthians 15:25-28)

In obedience to God, His people are overcoming the powers of Satan that control world systems. Absolutely every world system will collapse. The corruption of the world's most powerful agencies grows worse and worse. But in the midst of a failing economy, falling governments, unemployment, the devastation of cities with homelessness, poverty, crime and all the other social and political ills, the Kingdom of God rules in our hearts.

Christ's rule is confined to the spiritual realm until every system has been proven to be inadequate by the standards established through the witness of the Church. That standard demands that our economics be incontestable; our social relationships be impeccable; our families be harmonious; our work ethics be aimed at excellence; our attitudes be loving, compassionate and forgiving. God will judge the world not only by that man Christ Jesus, but also by the witness in demonstration of the Church.

What is the end of the history as we know it? Christ will take all those people and things subject to Him and present them to the Father. He will say, "Father, these are the ones who have lived in obedience to Me." With that final decree, the theocracy is established throughout the universe.

Then God will say to the powers of darkness, "I have proven that people with free will can choose obedience to Me. I have proven to you that your system of greed, violence and self-centeredness will fail. I will judge your corruption by the standard of their obedience to the rule of Christ."

Peter says that we will have a "new heaven and a new earth." The same word that Peter used for the earth "burning" is the Old Testament reference to "purging" the earth. The earth will be purged of world systems. The purging of all rebellion against God is demonstrated to the world by Christ and an obedient Church. Then God's judgment is swift and sure. Satan is put out of commission.

The difference between rebellion against God and obedience to God simplifies understanding the Kingdom of God. It simplifies identifying who God's people are. Every time you see rebellion in a child, you know that Satan's kingdom is winning in that child's life. Every time you see people making choices in their careers backed by prayer and spiritual counseling, you know that God's kingdom rules in their hearts. The Church, as never before, must learn and demonstrate submission to the Holy Spirit.

Throughout Church history, the Spirit of God has attempted to break through to bring God's people into revivals of obedience. Martin Luther led a revival of justification by faith. Nailing the 95 Theses to a church door was an act of an obedient man that triggered the purging process among God's people. That is the reason his movement is called "The Reformation."

God's messengers of that "Reformation" such as John Calvin, John Knox, George Whitfield and others preached a sound theology of repentance. The purging of Catholic indulgences and immoralities was God's response to the cry of those seeking Him who were being led astray. But I believe that many of the observances of sacraments that Protestants threw out along with all the corruption triggered an over-reaction. Many times in a great move, the pendulum swings too far.

For example, I do not believe that observing the Lord's Table or the sacrament of baptism are symbolic. I was taught as a child that baptism was "an outward sign of an inward grace." Such an understanding makes the sacrament of baptism optional—and I now do not believe that it is optional for the believer.

I will not argue the doctrine of transubstantiation in the Eucharist, but I will only quote Jesus' own words, "This is My body . . . this is My blood." The word "sacrament" means "mystery." I cannot—nor should I—attempt to explain what spiritual laws observing the sacraments set in motion. I only know by faith that something wonderful happens. I believe that in the observance of the Eucharist, we experience the real presence of Christ.

I also know that the Eucharist is central to unifying the body of Christ. Paul taught that many Christians die prematurely because they "do not properly discern the body of Christ." The Lord's table is a place of healing for relationships. It is a place of physical healing. It is a place to heal the wounded soul.

Should I venture even further? If a Christian does not have the covering of spiritual eldership in his or her life, he or she does not understand the Kingdom of God. Paul taught the early Church to "obey those over you in the Lord." Unless you have someone over you, what elder do you call when you are sick? How can the Church function as an effective army when all the soldiers serve as their own commanders?

We have many soldiers running loose, conducting their own campaigns and not accomplishing very much. They don't threaten the powers of darkness. How can they ever understand obedience to God without any concept of eldership? How can they enter the Kingdom while refusing to share in the witness of Christ's body on earth? Many are deceived because they do not discern the body of Christ.

What is "covenant" anyway? Covenant between Christ and His Church includes repentance, water baptism, celebrating the Eucharist, the counsel of spiritual eldership, observing the Sabbath and tithing unto the Lord. Christians who regard these steps in their Christian walk as optional do not comprehend God's Kingdom at all. They certainly do not understand the meaning of covenant.

Protestants did away with the confessional, and modern Christianity has been greatly deprived of consistent, deliberate confessing of our sins. We pray, "Forgive us our debts"—not sins! Too often dark sins are hidden in the heart. Eventually, the need to confess is undeniable when hidden problems surface or explode.

God gives a few, simple steps to help us understand obedience, and too many Christians disregard God's own criterion. Christians devise their own system of obedience to God. They say, "Hey! The man upstairs knows I'm not perfect! He's going to have mercy on me. I'll make it in!" Think again!

The power of the Holy Spirit is essential to living as a witness of the Kingdom of God. God's people need His power to carry out His will. Our witnessing to the Kingdom of God is far more than declaration; it is also demonstration. God will never judge the world until the Church lives an adequate demonstration of the standards of His Kingdom against world systems.

I say this with tremendous hesitation because I am a man

fully aware of my own weaknesses, but heads of denominations come to me to ask how my congregation is able to accomplish certain goals. Graduate classes from the Methodist seminary where I graduated send students to study the inner workings of our church. President George Bush asked me how we were able to bring people into racial harmony with one another. One simple answer: the Holy Spirit leads us.

The Kingdom is not about "churchology"; it is about the rule of Christ through the Holy Spirit within us. In the Holy Spirit, we know the righteousness, peace and joy that constitutes the Kingdom of God. When you live your life under the direction of the Holy Spirit, you no longer belong to yourself. You are a subject and citizen of God's Kingdom.

So where is the Holy Spirit moving today? The great Pentecostal outpouring that began around 1884 ushered in this final movement. The great Azusa Street revival and the outpouring in the mountains of Tennessee and Georgia that set on fire my dad and old Brother Tomlinson and F.J. Lechee and Brother Bryant and others I knew as a boy were the first stage. When they received the baptism in the Holy Spirit, they were turned out of Methodist, Baptist and Lutheran churches.

Did they leave those churches? No, dear! They were kicked out! But God began to build a strong army of Pentecostals. For the most part, they held little understanding of orthodox theology, but they knew the power of God. My dad only went to the third grade, and he memorized the Bible because he couldn't read, but he stood before European royalty as a mighty American preacher.

As the Pentecostal movement grew, it adopted Pharisaical rules of behavior. They set high standards for church member-

ship that scrutinized dress, entertainment and habits. They elim-
inated more people than they allowed to join them. The first
time I stood on the floor of their assembly as a young preacher,
I took issue with their rule against wearing wedding bands. I was
laughed off the stage and almost kicked out of the meeting. The
new Pharisees told God who could and who could not join their
churches.

I'll never forget the shock I experienced the first time I
preached in a Charismatic church. The Holy Spirit was falling on
women wearing makeup and jewelry! I stood there preaching to
a bunch of "Jezebels" sitting in the congregation, and I said,
"God, You must have made a mistake! You and I both know
that these women are going straight to hell, and yet they are
receiving the Holy Spirit!"

Very quietly, the Spirit of the Lord whispered to me, "No, this
is the way I am moving. I am taking down all your Pentecostal
Pharisaism to bring you to a greater understanding of My
Kingdom."

Then came the great Charismatic movement. Millions of
Roman Catholics received the baptism in the Holy Spirit. A few
years ago, I sat in a Roman Catholic/Pentecostal Dialogue
because of the great numbers of Catholics who had received
the Holy Spirit. We shared for several days on the theological
differences and similarities in our faith as members of Christ's
body.

All the Protestant denominations felt the impact of God's
pouring out His Spirit among their ranks. Thousands of Lutheran, Episcopalian, Presbyterian and Baptist pastors received the
baptism in the Holy Spirit. Charismatic prayer groups and
churches sprang up everywhere across the land. The new Char-

ismatics had much to learn from the old line Pentecostals, but they also had some valuable things to teach.

At last, Reformed theologians brought sound theology to be joined with the power of the Holy Spirit. God had given insight to theologians such as St. Augustine who wrote pure Kingdom theology in his *City of God.* For the first time Pentecostals were opened to the historical heritage of the church. Many aspects of Pentecostal theology needed correction. Some eschatological ideas had filtered into their theology that were totally unbiblical. Some literal interpretations of Scripture had been canonized in a way that led the Pentecostal movement astray.

God's move across the earth in this hour is the restoration of sound theology to His Church. We are being joined in our thinking to the Church fathers of previous generations who now form that cloud of witnesses in the spiritual realm. We are the continuation of their faithfulness and obedience to God's will to their generations. They are incomplete without us because together we form the eternal body of Christ.

And what follows the restoration of sound theology among God's obedient, Spirit-empowered people? Across the earth a spiritual hunger will grow like never before. We are in the beginning stages of a great harvest—prophesied for decades before the coming of the Lord. The "hungry" of the earth will include both Christians and non-believers ripe for our witness. Christians who have grown cold will begin to desire the fire of God in their lives as they have never known before.

The Berlin wall did not fall because of diplomatic genius or government instability. It fell because Spirit-filled believers knew how to pray for a wall to crumble. Now the Holy Spirit is moving back to inhabit those great cathedrals of Europe. They do not need "westernized Christianity" to awaken them—they need the power of the Holy Spirit.

So are you hungry? After preaching almost fifty years, I am more hungry for God now than when He called me to preach as a seventeen-year-old boy. I am on fire to know more and more about the Lord. The more I know, the more I realize how much there is to learn. The more I hear the Lord speaking, the more eager I become to hear His voice.

We are coming to a time in history when the Word of the Lord will be so alive that people will be healed of physical infirmities simply by hearing an anointed message. People will come to the table of the Lord to be healed physically and emotionally. We are about to experience "signs and wonders" like never before—IF God's people walk in obedience to Him. Only when we come into total obedience to God and His covenants, will He trust us with His power.

Today God's people are in a valley of decision. Some will make wrong choices. Some will fall. The Bible says that the eyes of the Lord go "to and fro," searching for hearts He can trust. What would you do if God trusted you with His supernatural power? Put up a sign for healing? Go on television?

God will find men and women in obedience to Him. The Pentecostal movement was powerful, but God is doing a new thing that will set the world on fire. The Charismatic movement was encompassing and inclusive, but God will extend His witness far and wide, as the waters cover the sea. This "new thing" will not come through intellect, training or knowledge of sound principles. It will come through the simple obedience of God's people. Simply that! And in ways you never anticipated, God is testing you to see whether you choose a path of rebellion, or the way of obedience that He has ordained through Christ for your life.

4 THE SOLUTION

N obody will argue with you that the world is in chaos. The whole world staggers under the weight of problems caused by rebellion against God throughout creation. Yet Jesus gave us the solution. God's people hold the "keys" that unlock His Kingdom of righteousness, peace and joy in the Holy Spirit that ensure overcoming the rule of darkness over the earth. So why the mess? One answer! The people of God must live, move and breathe as solution-oriented people by using the keys in their hands.

One day Peter spoke out a revelation to proclaim who Jesus was— "the Christ, the Son of the Living God" (Matthew 16:16). Jesus' response to Peter's insight is so profound that many

Christians miss the significance of what Jesus is saying to us today about who we are in this world.

Jesus replied, "And I also say to you that you are Peter. And upon this rock (the "rock" of revelation of who Jesus is), I will build My church, and the gates of Hades shall not prevail against it" (Matthew 16:18).

Then Jesus continues, "And I will give you the keys of the kingdom of heaven, and whatever you bind on earth will be bound in heaven, and whatever you loose on earth will be loosed in heaven" (Matthew 16:19). Do you live as if you have the keys to the Kingdom at your disposal?

God's people will give an account as to how they used the keys to the Kingdom. Jesus upbraided the Pharisees for standing in the doorway of the Kingdom—neither going inside themselves nor allowing others to enter. Some who criticize ministries bringing people into the revelation of God's Kingdom will be held accountable for their remarks. Ministries basing their decisions upon the opinions of people or fear of controversy or misunderstanding of Kingdom authority will be called into account. God will not allow His people to remain neutral in this vital hour of witness.

When you pray the Lord's Prayer ". . . Thy Kingdom come, Thy will be done on earth as it is in heaven," you are agreeing with Jesus that you have the keys to bind and loose in heaven and on earth. Too many Christians are simply reciting words without realizing what they are proclaiming!

Yes, God's rule is sovereign. But whenever He releases an area of sovereignty into mankind's responsibility, He limits Himself. Allow me to illustrate this. When I give the keys of our family's car to one of my daughters, she can drive that car anywhere she pleases. She can go shopping, dancing, to a bar or to a church. By giving her the keys, I have trusted her with my authority and my possession—trusting that she will make good decisions in driving and in choosing her destination.

God has done the same with us by giving us the keys to His Kingdom. He says in essence, "I own you, the car, the highway, but I will allow you to drive. You have free will in this assign-ment." God allows you and me to make decisions about our witness every day. You and I hold the keys to the Kingdom that either unlock the door to others, or keep out those we see and know on a daily basis.

The solution for this planet does not rest with God. God has done everything He will do. Jesus proclaimed "It is finished!" as He hung on the cross. Jesus rose from the dead and told His disciples to wait in Jerusalem until they were empowered by the Holy Spirit to take the Kingdom message around the world. Even the Holy Spirit, our Teacher, our Guide, is subject to the will of every Christian who chooses whether to yield or to resist His direction.

The solution for the earth is not with God—the solution is with you and me! That statement scares many Christians because they do not want to assume spiritual maturity. God will not act except through His people in these days of harvest. Why did Jesus tell us to pray for laborers if God didn't need us to harvest the earth? Too many Christians resist becoming the laborers that Jesus prayed they would be.

What are the circumstances by which God's people labor in the harvest today? God has given us the keys. We sit in seats of authority in heavenly places because the gates (authority) of hell cannot withstand us. Jesus Christ sits at the right hand of the

Father making intercession for us—ensuring that we cannot fail regardless of the accusations against us, our frailties of the flesh, our distractions or human errors. Jesus paid the price for all our sins at the cross—and both He and we must continually remind the devil of that fact.

Empowered by the Holy Spirit, we are the solution of God for the world. Is the crime rate soaring? Are public housing communities overflowing? Are drug traffic and the murder rate increasing? These problems exist because God's people are not living as the solution He has instructed them to be. Before the coming of Christ, the most intelligent, gifted, talented and wisest people on earth will be Spirit-filled believers who witness boldly to the rule and reign of Christ.

We have only begun to enter an age of restoring gifts and talents back to God's Church. We have called an end to the subtle deception of the enemy to rob the Church of talents like Nat King Cole's and Aretha Franklin's who began in the church and were lured away by the fame and fortune the world offered them. That trend is turning around. I listened to a young man sitting in my office recently telling me that he wanted to begin an agency to promote talented artists from the church to achieve successful careers in the world. I smiled as he shared his big ideas. Then I laid into him.

I informed him that we are entering a day when the world will line up to get into the church to hear the best, see the best and learn their lessons from anointed musicians and artists. I suggested that he go to the world and recruit the best talent he could find and bring them to Chapel Hill Harvester Church in Atlanta where they could make something out of their talent that will pay off for eternity!

We pray talented people into our church. Then we begin getting invitations to open the Braves games, to sing and dance at malls, to entertain with the Governor at Underground Atlanta, to sing for political rallies or to participate in the Martin Luther King, Jr. celebrations. Do we go? Of course! We go with the attitude, "The Kingdom of God has come nigh unto you!" We take that talent to the world—but we know we are using keys to unlock the Kingdom for whoever will enter.

Spirit-filled Christians should be the presidents, governors, senators and mayors in places of authority across our nation. Politics has become tainted with distrust because God's people have sounded retreat instead of marching forward. Anywhere quality living is an issue, God's people need to be the ones sitting at the head of the table with the most clout and the greatest boldness in projecting a plan. Do you realize that the Supreme Court has more influence upon your daily life than almost any other force in America? So who ought to be sitting on the Supreme Court?

I don't care whether you belong to the Democratic or the Republican party—that is not the issue. I refuse to be categorized politically—I am a Christian! The Bible instructs us to pray for those in authority over us. We need to hold them up in prayer daily and to minister to them every chance we get.

During the first few days of Operation Desert Storm, I was attending a meeting of pastors on the West Coast, and Billy Graham was supposed to join us for a few days of dialogue. He telephoned to say that he was spending some time with President Bush at the White House. That visit was not publicized, but I'm convinced that the prayers and faith of God's people made a tremendous difference in the outcome of that conflict. After my own conversation with President Bush about his faith in God, I am glad that such a man stood at the helm during this national crisis.

The Kingdom of God will ring around the world if we will follow God's instructions. We cannot be guided by human wisdom in such a critical day. Mankind's ideas will not solve anything. Scientists will not invent solutions to our problems. Educators will only educate people to come up with better ways to commit crimes and produce and distribute pornography. Politicians will confess that they don't have the answers. Federal spending (creating more and more debt) will not bail out our society.

> *Therefore, since all these things will be dissolved, what manner of persons ought you to be in holy conduct and godliness, looking for and hastening the coming of the day of God, because of which the heavens will be dissolved, being on fire, and the elements will melt with fervent heat? Nevertheless we, according to His promise, look for new heavens and a new earth in which righteousness dwells. Therefore, beloved, looking forward to these things, be diligent to be found by Him in peace, without spot and blameless.* (2 Peter 3:11-14)

God asks you, "If I have given you the keys, if the solution rests with you, what kind of person should you be?" You have the power to hasten the coming of the Lord—as awesome as that sounds. How? Your witness affects God's timing in purging and judging unrighteousness in the world. How are we "spotless and blameless" if we are sinners? God wants our spirits continually purified through Christ's atonement.

Too often the Church has emphasized righteous behavior instead of spiritual purity. Flesh problems were never the focus of Jesus' ministry. He zeroed in on people's rebellious hearts. People with great moral problems fell at Jesus' feet in repentance, while the Pharisees rejected Him. The same thing happens in the Church today. Some of the most morally "righteous" Christians miss the value of repentance, confession and mercy. They are so convinced that they are "good," that they can never be forgiven of their pride and hardheartedness. We must prepare ourselves—and then the world—for the coming of the Lord.

Those in the early Church were convinced that they would live to see the coming of the Lord, so the Apostle Paul began to prepare them for the possibility that some would die before Jesus returned:

> *Therefore, comfort one another with these words. But concerning the times and the seasons, brethren, you have no need that I should write to you. For you yourselves know perfectly that the day of the Lord so comes as a thief in the night. For when they say, "Peace and safety!" then sudden destruction comes upon them, as labor pains upon a pregnant woman. And they shall not escape. But you, brethren, are not in darkness, so that this Day should overtake you as a thief. You are all sons of light and sons of the day. We are not of the night nor of darkness. Therefore let us not sleep, as others do, but let us watch and be sober.* (1 Thessalonians 4:18-5:6)

When we meet Christ, we will experience a greater "rapture" than the wives who meet their husbands' ship after a war. We will be "caught up" with the thrill of meeting the bridegroom. In the parable of the five wise and the five foolish virgins, they went out to meet the bridegroom and then they went in to the marriage supper. What does the Apostle Paul tell the Church to do with the promise of this scene? He says that we should "comfort one another"—not build an eschatology.

The Church has focused upon flesh sins and eschatology more than on ways to use the keys they hold in their hands. The solution to the hopelessness of our planet lies with the keys we hold. The solution will never be found in doctrines, systems or organizations. The solution is in the keys we hold.

———————— So What is the Solution? ————————

1. **The Church must get clear signals.** We need to get our signals from the Holy Spirit. Often Jesus would say, "He who has ears to hear . . ." implying that not everyone who heard His teaching was listening with spiritual ears. I ask my congregation to touch their ears and pray for God to give them anointed ears to hear—especially if God has given me a "hard word" to deliver.

I can personally attest to the fact that some of my words have been totally distorted by those who hear with carnal ears. I am appalled at the content of what they claim to have heard me preach! So is my congregation who know me well, watch my ministry up close and hear me speak every week! When they read what I "supposedly" believe, they are as amazed as I am.

The consequences for getting the wrong signals can be quite serious. I was challenged by one noted critic only a few months before his death. He was writing some totally erroneous interpretations of my teaching, calling me a false prophet. Matters of life and death rest with God, and those who make judgments over ministries must be extremely careful with their words.

The ministry of God to the world can never be accomplished by the arm of the flesh. The Holy Spirit must give the signals and call the plan. By His Spirit—not by might, power, programs, ingenuity, schemes, marketing—but by His Spirit. When we are led by the Spirit, our programs and our marketing plans work—but not until God leads us.

We must pray by the power of the Holy Spirit. I know how to pray for a sick child or with someone to receive salvation, but in many circumstances, I simply do not know how to pray. The language of the Holy Spirit intercedes for us. I pray publicly for people to understand and agree with me before the Lord, but I rarely pray that same way in private. I pray in my spiritual language. I want God's perfect will with very clear signals. What if I am asking amiss? What if my own agenda gets in the way of what God wants to accomplish through me?

Clear signals from God never come through your intellect or listening to tapes of great preachers or flipping a coin. Clear signals come from open communication between you and God. Think of the families that could be saved if men and women knew how to get clear signals from God. God uses spiritual counselors, His Word, anointed sermons and those who love you in Christ to help you find His direction. But your primary confidence rests in your own inner assurance that you have made the right decision.

2. The Church must sanctify herself to prepare for the great things that God is ready to do. God will not use an unclean vessel. Men of God like Joshua would go before the nation of Israel and tell them, "Sanctify yourselves! God wants to do great things!"

God does not respond to world events as He responds to the obedience of His people. That concept is often lost by our thinking that the headlines are more important to God than the way we live our lives. Wrong! Jesus spent His time with ordinary people to whom He gave an extraordinary mission.

God promises, ". . . if my people, who are called by My name will humble themselves, and pray and seek My face, and turn from their wicked ways, then I will hear from heaven, and will forgive their sins and heal their land" (2 Chronicles 7:14). This verse—quoted so frequently—underscores the principle that God's people are the keys to His interaction with earth.

Worldly governments do not hold the keys to God's intervention in worldly events. The ones whom God hears are His people. Banking systems do not wield control over the earth's resources—God's people do! If God's people sanctify themselves and prepare for God to move through them, He will release His power through His people as the Church has never known before.

Intercession before the Lord is causing many governments to change hands. People are crying for freedom at the risk of their lives because the Spirit of the Lord is moving across the land. Perilous times cause the instability that we are experiencing in governments around the world, but the end of the matter is absolutely glorious. God's Word instructs us to live pure, clean, holy lives in such a perilous day.

So what is a life of holiness? When I was growing up, it meant no makeup, hair down to your fanny and no jewelry. Somehow we missed the fact that many of those "holy" people were mean and self-righteous. They drove their children away from God with their sharp tongues. They didn't care about other people at all. They closed sinners out of the church and gossiped about them.

Today, you can have a little girl run around looking like a Jezebel, and you wonder if she will ever get close to God. Before you know it, that girl will touch God and change a whole community. Some people stand around saying, "Hold it, God! Didn't You see how she was dressed?"

Do you know what God does? He takes the throwaways and does a better job than most of us to show us that He doesn't need our approval. A rooster or a donkey could preach better messages than any minister if God decides to use one of them. God doesn't want to make us feel unimportant to Him, but all He needs is someone who will open his or her heart to His will. All God wants is someone who will say, "God, You have given me an opportunity to do something for You!"

Holiness and sanctification is the condition of one's heart. We sanctify ourselves by opening our lives totally to God. We sanctify ourselves by guarding our witness from any thoughts, words or deeds that would bring shame to the Lord. We sanctify ourselves through a weeding-out process of negative emotions and negative influences so that we are totally free to hear and to follow the Holy Spirit.

Are you ready to go every week into a public housing community? Are you willing to teach a forty-five-year-old man to read? Will you help a single mother with three children to write a resume for her first job? Will you work with young boys—most from broken homes—in a sports program? Will you be willing to use the keys you hold any way that God tells you to use them?

3. The Church must get serious about the harvest. Jesus said that the Kingdom was like a merchant seeking beautiful pearls. The merchant found one pearl of great price, and he sold all that he had to purchase it (Matthew 13:45). That pearl is the truth of God's Kingdom. That truth is worth everything and anything. It may cost you friends, denominational ties, or those things that are dearest to you.

The rich young ruler got inspired by listening to Jesus talk about the Kingdom, and he ran up to Him. He asked Jesus, "Tell me what I need to do to get in on all this great 'abundant living and eternal life' You're talking about, Jesus."

Jesus answered him, "You know what the Law says to do."

He replied, "Oh, I've done all that—no "R"-rated movies, no drinking, no cigarettes, no wild women . . ."

Jesus looked deep into his eyes, "Go sell everything you have and give it to the poor and come, follow Me."

"Wait a minute, Jesus! I've got a Jaguar! I have important associates in the world that I need to impress. Do you know how much I spend on one suit? You don't realize what you've told me to do!"

Does Christ rule in your life? That young man walked away sorrowfully because he would not pay the price. Many will walk away sorrowfully. Others will say to God, "I'll do whatever you say—no matter what it costs me!" And God will begin to work through them in ways they never imagined.

How does Christ rule in your life? Does He govern your deci-sions? Are you in the place of service where He wants you to be? Your spiritual leaders are called by the Lord to equip you for the work of the Kingdom. You have an assignment.

Members of my congregation will come to me with great ideas for ministry. They will outline some plan to me, and then I'll say to them, "Great! When are you going to start?" They know not to tell me their ideas unless they are willing to do the work.

If God gives you an idea, get going! God gave you the idea, and once it has been submitted through the proper channels in the church leadership, you need to begin making that idea to become reality. When the rule of Christ reigns in your life, you will find your place of service.

4. **The Church must give clear signals.** When we receive clear signals from God, follow the leading of His Spirit and get serious about the harvest, then we must give clear signals our-selves. One of the major problems in the world today is that God's people are giving mixed signals. We preach unity and can't even hold our families together. We tell the world about the love of Jesus Christ, and we can't even get along with other church members or the pastor. The church staff works in con-tinuous bickering, turmoil and confusion. Pastors can't even work on meeting some community needs with the pastor of the church across the street.

If God sends an anointed messenger to a city to give a mes-sage from Him to the spiritual leaders, most of them will fail to show up. They never think of asking God whether they should go hear His messenger—they will check their calendars. Then their churches start to die. Their families get into trouble. They will find themselves up against the wall in situations, and they cry, "God! What is going on here? What is happening? Why are things falling apart?"

Jonah told the men on the ship about to sink in a storm, "Throw me off, and you'll be all right." When God sends a messenger, you had better be careful about the surroundings of that man. I never invite someone to speak to my congregation without being sure that I'm getting the right signals from God about that messenger. I am accountable for their spiritual well-being, and I don't want for them to miss an opportunity or to be lead down the wrong path.

Jesus addressed the people hearing the right signals.

> *But to what shall I liken this generation? It is like children sitting in the marketplaces calling to their companions saying, "We played the flute for you, and you did not dance; We mourned for you, and you did not lament." For John came neither eating nor drinking, and they say, "He has a demon." The Son of Man came eating and drinking, and they say, "Look, a glutton and a winebibber, a friend of tax collectors and sinners!" But wisdom is justified by her children.* (Matthew 11:16-19)

John came in a life-style of total discipline, and he was criticized. Jesus came in a life-style of compassion and inclusive love that reached out to people in trouble, and He was also criticized. The people didn't know the signals. One day they were insisting upon the prophet feasting, and for the next prophet they were advocating fasting.

The people wanted to play the flute and watch their spiritual leaders dance to their tunes. The Bible teaches that God appoints a time for all things: fasting, feasting, dancing, mourning, standing still, planting, reaping, being born and dying. Clear signals come by listening to the Holy Spirit and following His directions.

I'm going to take the liberty to brag on the members of Chapel Hill Harvester Church. If a messenger comes among us who does not give a clear signal, my congregation will love that person, listen politely to their song or message, perhaps even clap their hands and sing along—but they know the difference between anointing and performance!

They won't say anything—even to one another—but they will discern the spirit of that minister with absolute accuracy. Spiritually mature people will hear clear signals of the Holy Spirit. When unclear signals are given, people don't know whether to fast or cry or dance. Ministry falls apart. But if the Church is to be that shining witness that God is calling us to be in this hour, the Church must receive and give clear signals.

We cannot afford merely to guess what is God's will for us in this day. Every prophecy that I speak to the people in my congregation in Atlanta is recorded and verified over time to confirm it. Old Testament prophets were stoned for declaring a false word. If we still practiced stoning today, many Charismatic congregations would get the microphone out of the aisles of their churches. Stoning would certainly purify the mixture of flesh and spirit we hear in many "words of God" given today.

We must be as wise as serpents. Anyone who speaks a "thus saith the Lord" needs to be ready to stand by that word with his or her life. A word from God is either "yea" or "nay" without variation or compromise. We shouldn't be dissecting a prophecy later by saying, "This part was right on; this part was wrong—and said for this reason." Until correction in this area of ministry filters throughout the Body of Christ, the Church can have no confidence in giving or receiving clear signals.

We need to be tactful in speaking to an unsaved, unredeemed world. They need to hear from God in their own language—even if it sounds like marketing or advertising initially. The language of this generation has tuned people's ears to respond to a certain sound. The reverse is also true. Churches have spoken in "King James" English for too long, and our "thous" and "thys" close people's ears. The world has learned the key to getting people's attention—give them something; serve them in some way; offer them a fresh idea or approach to solving a problem.

The relevance of our message is based upon how to address "new battlefields" that plague modern society. What are we going to do about drugs? How are we going to preach to the poor and homeless in our own streets? How are we going to make governments realize that it is "the hearts" of people, and not legislation, that will combat racism? Busing people for integration didn't work! Except for a few pockets of true integration, we are still a segmented, divided society—even on Sunday mornings in God's house.

I spoke recently to a group of spiritual leaders in Washington state. When I got off the plane, I sensed in my spirit a tremendous oppression over that city. I realized, without knowing one single fact about the area, that this city was gripped by strong racial prejudices. As I rode through the city, I saw signs on churches—Cambodian, Spanish, black churches, lily white churches. I thought, "My God, here is more prejudice than we have in the South!"

The world will never understand the Prince of Peace as long as we who serve Him are so divided. It's time we wised up to the devices of the enemy. We still stew in prejudice and believe that God will bless us! The most segregated hour of the week is still on Sunday morning at 11:00. But some have gotten their signals corrected. God is pouring out His Spirit upon those who know how to be themselves totally, yet blend themselves with other members of Christ's body.

My congregation of more than twelve thousand members is almost equally balanced along racial lines. Black members of my church love me because I was ready to go to prison or die for them in the '50s when it wasn't popular for a white, southern preacher to call for unity. That message has shaped my ministry. Blacks and whites in our church learn from one another and the cultural blending has made us the witness that we are.

For example, I was raised in south Georgia where we cried, snotted and sneezed at funerals just as those in black churches do traditionally. I began teaching my members how to celebrate the "homegoing" of their loved ones. We began to talk about crying and carrying on and reading every name on every wreath, and so on. The focus of funerals shifted to celebrating the life of that person who is now with the Lord instead of mourning the loss of him or her. Why are people willing to change their cultural traditions? They trust me as a father who loves them and wants them to know life from God's perspective.

Governments and laws will never do that. Government solves problems by building another housing project, increasing welfare funds, and in the process government takes away people's motivation, dignity and ingenuity. Welfare is a product of hell itself. If the Church were doing its job properly, we would never need welfare! Government agencies would be coming to God's people and saying, "What do you need the governor to do in this situation?"

Wouldn't that be marvelous! I believe that if we get on track, that dream will become a reality in our generation. But we cannot be afraid or paranoid when opportunities arise to be bold for the Lord. God's Word instructs us to pray for boldness. Evangelists in the early church were being beaten and thrown into prison every day. Do you know what they prayed for? Not deliverance—they prayed for boldness!

God does not instruct us to pray for deliverance from our circumstances. We are being trained to be overcomers. We overcome with a bold testimony to the power of Jesus Christ. Every day we need to be walking into the places where Satan has established his stronghold and boldly raising up the banner of Jesus by saying, "Devil, you don't belong in this place anymore! Your time is up!"

Don't tell me it won't work! I've seen it work repeatedly! The devil knows who you are, especially when you begin to step on his turf. Just be sure that you are registered in heavenly places before you begin putting Satan on the run. We have ministered to patients from mental institutions brought to our church for deliverance under armed guard. Know your level of ministry and be bold in whatever place God has placed you for service.

The Church will face devastation unless we stir up our boldness now. I'm reminded of a story Charles Colson records in one of his books, *Kingdoms In Conflict.* He told of Martin Niemoller and Dr. Dietrich Bonhoeffer, two German pastors who were imprisoned by Hitler during World War II. When Hitler first came to power, the church was busy doing its thing and didn't pay him too much attention.

Martin Niemoller said that they came for the Communists first, but Christians weren't Communist, so they remained silent. Then they came for the Jews, but Christians weren't Jews, so they remained silent. Then they came for members of the trade unions, but most Christians didn't belong to trade unions, so they remained silent. They came for Catholics, but most German Christians weren't Catholic, so they didn't speak up. One day those who had been silent heard a knock at their own doors, and no one was left to speak for them (Charles Colson, *Kingdoms In Conflict*, Zondervan Publishing House; 1987, p. 125).

So how bold are you? How loud is your voice? God has given us keys, solutions, power and zeal. He has promised that all things are possible if we believe. Faith means action. We can hope to receive God's promises to us, which are held eternally in a heavenly treasure chest. We put our faith into action to see that hope realized on earth.

We offer the solutions from God with great love and compassion. Jesus never ministered until He was filled with compassion for those whom He touched. God will not release His power until He finds men and women who have tender hearts.

> *Remember the prisoners as if chained with them—*
> *those who are mistreated—since you yourselves are*
> *in the body also.* (Hebrews 13:3)

That verse means that someone in bondage to alcohol makes me to experience that bondage as I go to free him. I must feel the chains of divorced people before I can help restore them to wholeness again. I must feel the chains of people living in public housing before I can help them to find solutions economically and socially. Every time someone is mistreated because of their gender or race, age or class distinction, I must feel that injustice also before I can crusade against it.

When the church is moved with compassion, we will have open doors to give solutions to the world. God will open them. People know the difference in patronization and compassion. As a child, the experience of seeing a young, handsome, black field hand shot to make him work harder has never left my mind. I vowed then to do something about racial injustice, and I have kept that vow through more than forty years of ministry.

True compassion cannot be conjured up or imitated. It must be real to get results. True compassion begins by being honest with ourselves about our own prejudices, doubts and motives. God will put you in places to test your motives and your prejudices. You will find yourself in shocking situations. You will need to stretch spiritually—faith, hope and love!

But as God releases His compassion within you, you will be healed and restored as you minister healing to others. That summarizes the source of solutions for a hurting world. The Spirit of the Lord is upon you to preach to the poor to get them out of poverty; to bind up the wounds of broken-hearted people; to set captives of drugs, habits or crime free from spiritual bondages; to cause people blinded by prejudice, guilt or sin to see again; to give hope and life to those under a weight of oppression; and to boldly proclaim that the Kingdom of God is at hand to anyone who will grab hold of it in this hour of destiny!

You hold the keys. What are you going to do with them?

5 Operation Homefront

Some time ago, the Lord told me to go to Grant Park in Atlanta to see the Cyclorama. I am a student of history, and I had seen the Cyclorama—a circular painting depicting the battle in Atlanta during the Civil War—many times. I went that day under the Holy Spirit's direction, and I walked around wondering what I was supposed to learn from the experience.

As the battle on the canvas was being explained by a narrator, a light focused upon General Grant sitting on top of a mountain overlooking the conflict in progress below him. God spoke clearly to my spirit and said, "That's it! That's where I have you right now."

I understood instantly what God meant. I have not made

myself the overseer of a great church in Atlanta. I have not put myself in a place where I watch the battle raging over God's plan for the earth. God has put me there. My life now centers upon viewing the action from afar, watching what is going on and interceding before God over the ministry I am called to lead.

At Chapel Hill Harvester Church, as in many thousands of churches around the world today, there is tremendous hunger for the things of the Lord. The twenty-five associate pastors who help me in the work of the ministry every day are hungry for God. They fast and seek the Lord's direction with me on a regular basis. They understand the tremendous battles over our church as we seek to fulfill God's purposes for us.

Our school leaders have an enormous desire to see children and youth come into the full measure of faith that God has for them. These educators hunger for a genuine move of God throughout our educational institutions. They pray daily over our students and pour themselves out in tenderness and caring love as well as impart academic knowledge.

I meet weekly with the media staff to be sure they grasp where our ministry is headed, and what God has instructed us to convey outside the walls of our church. They must be tuned to my spirit if we are to reach nations by television and publications to share the deposit of God in this local church that God has raised up to touch other local churches.

I pray daily over the staff of our ministry that God will stir up the hunger within them. That refining process must be continuous if we are to serve people with the excellence, purity and love that God honors in the work of the ministry. I ask the Lord to strengthen the weak places and use mightily those places in our staff operation that are strong.

Recently, God led me through a time of great discipline in fasting and seeking Him, and I thought I had come to the end of it. I sat watching a magnificent Easter production that our department of Worship and Arts was presenting as I thought, "Praise God! I have gone through a time of strict discipline, and now I can enjoy the fruit of it." Many wonderful rewards were already beginning to happen at our church! Excitement hung in the air! So many people were experiencing the fires of revival in their lives.

Immediately the Spirit of the Lord interrupted my pleasant thoughts. "You are in the middle of a battle, and you are not at the end of it. You must continue now until Pentecost." I felt my heart drop. But after a moment, I recovered to realize that God had just promised me a major victory only a few weeks away. I would rather hear a word from God calling me to strict discipline than to sit around in an euphoric state of false security.

Whenever a leader of God's people fasts and seeks Him, spirits surface to attack, distract or confuse that leader. The deeper God's people go into spiritual understanding, spirits such as negativism, rejection and jealousy always surface. Not sometimes—always! Fasting will surface both good and bad spirits in a ministry. Good spirits can surface during this time to begin a fruitful work for God.

During this continued discipline, I spoke to the youth of our church at their evangelistic outreach meeting called BEAM. Spirits began surfacing as I spoke to those young people. I was still ministering after midnight to people who had been dishonest and knew that because my discernment was at such a level, if they did not come forward, I would point them out. I was in no mood for playing their games.

In the late '70s and the early '80s, God raised up a mighty move among youth called Alpha. This move gave young people a spiritual option to the drug culture. They had wanted to get high on something. Music took them soaring away from reality. Satan had used rock-and-roll to deceive a generation about the meaning of life. Rock stars were satanic evangelists.

At the time, music was inseparable from the drug culture. Thousands of kids flocked to stadiums to get high together. Many who came to the Lord through the Alpha ministry would tell me privately, "You've never heard music until you are high on marijuana. It opens your ears to music you have never heard before."

So God raised up Alpha as a spiritual answer to the drug culture. Among those who found the Lord during that great move, some turned back to drugs. A few who had come out of that bondage even attempted to minister under the influence of those chemicals they had been delivered from. God spoke clearly. He would not allow such abomination in His name.

God ended the movement of Alpha, and many could not understand what had happened to the vehicle God had used to bring them to Himself. Many continued to grow spiritually, get married, have families and serve the Lord. Others turned back to the dead-end corruption they had known before Alpha had opened their lives to God's reality.

Youth today are not looking for a high. Times have changed. Today young people are searching for a reason—meaning and purpose—for life. The greatest cause of death among teenagers is suicide. A spirit of death hovers over the youth of our world today. Why does death have such open reception among them?

They come from broken homes, broken circumstances, hypocritical adults telling them what to do, and a lack of purpose for living.

Statistically, more than half of all teenagers have seriously considered suicide. As a pastor I know that what these teenagers are trying to say is that they desperately need help. Few of them really want to die. They are crying out for love and attention that will give them some hope.

The spirit of death drives youth to try odd and unusual sexual perversions. The spirit of death drives people to pornography so that they can feel some reaction, some response. The spirit of death drives them to life-threatening challenges. They require a high degree of stimulation to feel alive at all.

Unless the Church awakens to this challenge, we will have as many funerals for youth in the next five years as for the elderly. Christian parents will cry, "My God! I never knew my child was oppressed by a spirit of death!" Youth leaders must become aware of the battle, or they will waste time on social activities instead of giving youth purpose for living. As never before, young men and women must be involved with God's cause and His challenge to their lives at a very young age.

God is changing the paradigm of the ministry of the local church. There is a dramatic shift in our perspective. Our church in Atlanta began as a place of refuge to help people who were seekers of the Spirit. People joined our church with a "seekers" mentality. People flocked to their pastors' offices seeking a word from God. They faithfully attended our Tuesday morning service, "Life and Growth in the Spirit," seeking a word from God. Many lives were totally changed for the Lord by those who sought His will with all their hearts.

VESSELS OF THE HOLY SPIRIT

But now God is changing the focus. Now God wants people to understand their identities as "vessels of the Holy Spirit" instead of merely "seekers of God." What is the purpose and meaning of being "a vessel"? A vessel carries God's presence into the world and becomes a channel, or door, for others to find Him. When a group begins to identify themselves as vessels, they operate as a missionary society instead of people coming to get their needs met.

I must quickly add—as a vessel of the Holy Spirit—your needs will be met! But your motivation has shifted. Your needs are met as a by-product of serving others. Instead of going to services to get a spiritual lift, you take someone with you who needs encouragement, and thereby, you are encouraged also! You don't go to church to find a mate or get contacts for a job. You go as a missionary to help someone there who needs a job or a relationship.

God has given me a master plan of strategy for ministry in the city of Atlanta that I believe will work anywhere. Every local church is responsible for the city where God has placed them. Our strategy for ministry over that city must be as precise as military strategy in war. We need the air force, the ground troops, the sea support—all are important to our strategy as we work toward one common goal.

God's strategy for cities is called OPERATION HOMEFRONT. Your homefront is wherever you are. It can be in any nation of the earth. HOMEFRONT includes your family and their care. It certainly includes your own life and finding a place of service to

92

use your talents to fulfill your mission. But most of all, OPERA-TION HOMEFRONT refers to the mission of a local church to influence its community.

In 1986, God spoke to me as I looked out a hotel window overlooking the Capitol in Washington, D.C. about a worldwide agreement of prayer called "Let My Spirit Go." That year on July 4th, Christians prayed against the spirits of atheism, lawlessness and mammon at government buildings in every state in the U.S., on the Capitol steps in Washington, D.C., at the Statue of Liberty, and on other sites of governments in nations around the world. We agreed together in binding those ruler spirits.

Many churches and Christian groups joined in agreement in that prayer. Did those words binding those spirits of atheism, lawlessness and mammon make any difference in the world? Certainly many people have prayed for years over world events that have shaken nations at their foundations recently. But yes, I do believe that our agreement has made an impact in heavenly places and has been realized in actual events.

What stronghold sustained the wall in Berlin? That wall represented the atheistic philosophy of life. Now there is reported to be a tremendous revival of Christian faith in nations like Russia and Eastern Bloc countries that have based their political ideologies on atheism. The spirit of atheism has been bound—and we must continue to bombard heavenly places to see its total fall.

What is the message in the international outcry against law-less leaders in Panama, Iraq, the Philippines? The spirit of law-lessness has been exposed in those nations at the top of the government structure. How was it that police brutality has been exposed? Do you think it's accidental that some little home video camera picked up a scene of lawlessness within the framework of the law in Los Angeles recently? No! Christians have declared war on lawlessness in heavenly places!

And the spirit of mammon is in big trouble! Consumers are not spending as they once did—the credit system is increasingly frowned upon by the general public. The Savings and Loan scandals have infuriated people who have lost everything to greedy swindlers. People are incensed that our national debt is beyond comprehension.

The world economy is collapsing as nations like the U.S. and Russia go deeper and deeper into debt to Japan, putting foreigners in the position to call the policy on international trade for nations considered to be super-powers. Mammon—once all-powerful—has been challenged at its foundation.

God has given us the power to bind and loose spirits. We have the keys. In "Let My Spirit Go," we challenged those forces, powers and principalities in the heavenlies. Now we are beginning that same challenge against the spirit of death over our teenagers. But we need spiritual agreement in binding and loosing. The division in the Christian community has been orchestrated by powers of darkness to prevent our coming into this kind of agreement. Hell knows it cannot win when we use our keys in agreement with one another.

From the binding of those spirits, we move to ground operation. That's the way a victorious war is waged. We move from air strikes to ground force attacks. God has given us brilliant textbook strategy in waging war to fight in the real battle between spiritual light and darkness.

So let's look at the ground forces in OPERATION HOME-FRONT. First, we must recognize our problems. You cannot know the solution until you know the problem. We had to recognize that problem with Alpha. We are addressing the problems with teenagers in our church now. We are dealing with situations on our staff that need attention so that those not called by the Lord here will find their places of service elsewhere.

Our cities lie in waste. If most people knew the inner workings of their city government, they would be appalled. The political pressures and stroking to get certain people's pet projects in the spotlight are commonplace. Those in authority often cannot agree on a workable plan. They cannot even agree on identifying the problems, much less the solutions. True leaders are rare, while officials play politics with the lives of those believing that someone is in control and governing in their best interests.

Families are threatened with disintegration. Even good Christian men and women are headed for the divorce courts. People in ministry live in crumbling marriages. Children grow up in one-parent families in record numbers. Because of the overwhelming statistics of family disintegration, the courts have redefined the family from its traditional model. Family life—that bastion of learning principles of God's grace and love—no longer exists even in Christian homes.

Youth need artificial stimulation to make them feel alive. They are dead inside. Only some obsession—music, athletics, sex—brings them temporarily out of the state of deadness. They do not comprehend the ultimate meaning of life. They do not even desire purpose—much less search for it. Nothing matters. Not even their own lives!

Do I even need to alert the middle class that in a matter of weeks—only cut off from two or three months of paychecks—

they could be one of the homeless walking the streets? I have prophesied for years that one day an economic battle between the "haves" and the "have nots" will ignite across America. Idle words? I wish they were!

The welfare program has never been a solution to those needing basic necessities in life. The answer to welfare goes far deeper than economics. People need to address issues concerning their self-images, their sense of purpose, their talents and their skills. Family issues must be addressed before welfare recipients are really helped. People must be given hope to press beyond the symptoms of poverty. To remedy the reality of poverty, you must begin inside people's minds and spirits.

And what about the ominous plague of our day—AIDS? We've only seen the beginning. Many nations around the world are in the thralls of the kind of devastation that threatens this nation's future. People smugly believe that widely distributed information and available condoms will solve the problem, and we're only fooling ourselves. This disease is no longer confined to a specific group. AIDS is a HOMEFRONT problem.

I could go on and on describing the problems. Every person alive today understands that we are all engaged in this war—like it or not! God is calling for ground troops. Your battlefield is your community, your neighborhood, your own household.

My battlefield primarily has been designated by the Lord to be the city of Atlanta. I realize that some people may believe that assignment to be extremely presumptuous. Nevertheless, God has confirmed repeatedly that Chapel Hill Harvester Church has been blessed by the Lord because we are a spiritual laboratory to prove some things will work in a local church. Why? Because we are so great? No! We simply have agreed to allow God to experiment with us in some bold, innovative ministry. We'll go anywhere and try anything that God tells us to do.

And I might add that the innovative ministry I am referring to is under a microscope as well as in a spotlight. We are carefully scrutinized by friends and foes alike. We have been the subject of special news reports in every genre of the Atlanta press, and in the national news in numerous written articles and television news stories.

The international exposure is absolutely amazing to me. The German magazine *GEO* has featured us as "the church of the 21st Century" in its June, 1991 issue. The Asahi National Broadcasting Company headquartered in Tokyo (comparable to NBC in the U.S.) sent a Japanese television crew to attend our Easter morning services (1991) and interview me for a television special on "America: After the War." We are the subject of academic papers presented at seminars at the University of Calgary in Alberta, Canada, by researchers in the Department of Anthropology. And this exposure is only a report of the past few weeks.

So please don't think I'm being presumptuous. I am humbled, grateful and amazed that God would trust me with this kind of responsibility. I get letters every day from pastors all over the world asking me to come address their nations, but I know God has called me to make ministry work here in the city of Atlanta first. I have nothing to share with anyone unless OPERATION HOMEFRONT can influence Atlanta to know the Source of quality living. I won't tell you what to do until I've seen it work!

THE DIVISIONS OF OPERATION HOMEFRONT

Everyone fits in somewhere in the ground troop army of the Lord. All are necessary for our victory in this war. As vessels of the Holy Spirit, you are giving yourself to God as a living sacrifice to do His work in your community. In exchange for giving Him your life as a good soldier, He will recognize you in heavenly places before the Father (Mark 8:38). I believe that Christians around the world are ready to march once they get their orders. Okay! Here's the plan! See where you need to enlist:

1. Prayer Watch

Your pastor cannot appoint prayer warriors. A pastor cannot assign people to pray. The Spirit of the Lord raises up prayer warriors and a pastor can confirm them and recognize them, but they are called by God as much as that pastor is called. Those jumping into the Prayer Watch ministry who are self-serving will suffer greatly. I need to give you that warning.

God raises up intercessors over His cause—not just one person, but many. People called to this division will open their homes for intercessors to gather and pray over individuals, ministries and cities. They will never feel burdened by this ministry—they will eagerly pursue it with joy. If these homes become gossip stations, there will be death to that household. In God's service, that Prayer Watch home will be greatly blessed.

What does God assign to the Prayer Watch? Their sensitivity will be so keen that they will know their assignments. For some, it will be a situation or issue of a television news report that they will commit to prayer. Some will be assigned key individuals in other divisions of OPERATION HOMEFRONT whom they will cover and empower by agreement over the opportunities that person/people enter.

Pastors and heads of ministries seldom experience the kind of faithful prayer covering they need to make the impact that God wants us to make upon our communities. Christian teachers have such an opportunity to determine the future of our society if they only have adequate prayer support to open their witness to young, impressionable minds.

Those called to Prayer Watch will never turn loose. They will understand the meaning of tenacity and diligence until the mission is accomplished. This is not a calling for a few days or months; this is a life calling. Commitment over some matter or person will be until God releases that Prayer Watch soldier to another assignment. They may go home to be with the Lord after only one, life-long prayer assignment. Release can only come from God.

So many young families need these intercessors to commit themselves to pray over their decisions in a world where marriages are so fragile. A member of the Prayer Watch could commit themselves to one family in trouble, and watch God restore that home. Marriages are destroyed through great temptations because that couple has no covering of a Prayer Watch.

All persons in a visible ministry—such as pastors, teachers, singers or worship leaders—need someone to commit themselves specifically to pray for those individuals. They are so often targets of the enemy in an attempt to bring shame upon ministries.

Some members of OPERATION HOMEFRONT will dedicate their lives to praying for the mayor and city leaders. Some will call out the names of City Council members to God every day.

Some will join together to pray over the U.S. Supreme Court, the Congress and the President. Call their names. Follow their activities and pray over their individual needs.

The list is endless. Churches need people to commit their lives to praying over the finances of the ministry. Every church staff needs a Prayer Watch over them. I long for the day when I can see a chart that I can agree with in my own spirit as I read it— "A prayer group at 72 Capital Avenue is praying on Thursdays for _____. If God gives you an assignment for that particular person, family, group, ministry, come join us."

2. Ground Breakers

Ground Breakers prepare the soil through praise and worship. Unless they are carrying out their orders from God, our seeds for harvest just lie upon hard ground. Ground Breakers are never called to become famous "stars." That microphone in their hand, that instrument they hold, is a weapon used in God's service, not to serve themselves!

Ground Breakers go before the rest of the Operation to prepare the way. Their praise must be genuine. Their worship must be based upon true relationship with the Lord. People will spot the fakes. People will never follow behind those who are not engaged in true worship. Their own lives are at risk if they go into battle without a sure sound.

I have seen too many singers and artists become performers instead of worshipers. They lose their anointing, their self-images, they wander from pillar to post, and then try to lead worship! It just won't work.

The orchestra playing before a service begins, the singers opening a service, the music before a messenger comes to speak— all of these are assigned to break ground. When an anointed Spirit-filled singer opens a ball game by singing the National Anthem, or "God Bless America" at a political rally, he is not there to become a star, but to break ground for ministry. If people do not understand his purpose, all that seed will die right there. Opportunity is lost. God's purposes are aborted.

On the other hand, those songs of praise under the anointing can break hard, fallow ground as nothing else can! Anointed songs cause oppressive spirits to lose their grip. They open people to see, hear and understand. They teach and reinforce the words of God's messengers.

3. Door Keepers

God places Door Keepers in key places to relate to the secular world. They know how to speak the world's language. They know how to carry the ball and gain ground in the war. They use the influence given to them for some totally unrelated reasons to open doors for ministry.

Like the little handmaiden in the house of Naaman, they are in the right place at the right time to say, "I know someone who can help you find the answers to this problem." Without knowing when or how, Door Keepers understand that they occupy some place of influence that will be used by the Lord at the significant time to accomplish His purposes.

Our church in Atlanta has Door Keepers in key positions in city government, law enforcement, at the Mayor's office, etc. We have Door Keepers who work in influential positions in the local and national media. We have Door Keepers who serve in elected political offices. Door Keepers may relate to secular educational institutions in places of influence. They may serve on committees and boards of great social prominence. They may be professional athletes. They may have powerful positions in corporations.

These Door Keepers remain sensitive to God's purposes in their lives because they know their influence and success is to serve the Kingdom of God—not themselves. They understand the purpose of their opportunities. God will show them what to do. They will take risks. They will face opposition, but they will gain ground.

4. The Action Army

The final group of ground forces is the Action Army. These are the troops who march into the enemies' territory and fight battles by the power of the Holy Spirit. Their strategy is love. They move into areas such as athletics, or public housing, or literacy classes, or AIDS clinics to minister hope and solutions.

Our church has many of the Action Army in place, but the need for numbers of people to join this group has no limit. We have barely scratched the surface. The Action Army fights in hand-to-hand combat by looking people in the eyes and saying, "You don't need to give up! God is going to give your life purpose and meaning, and I'm here to help you find it!"

The Action Army may be service-oriented by working on construction, keeping the grounds or repairing someone's car. They meet needs and defeat the enemy's grasp upon people's lives and circumstances. They may keep children for a single mother to work. They may help her get a job. They may care for an elderly person. They may offer someone a place to stay until he or she can find a suitable home. They stay tuned to God to address the needs, hurts and possibilities in people and situations they pass by every day.

────── Attacking the Enemy at Home ──────

For OPERATION HOMEFRONT to work, all the divisions must be functioning and strong. All the divisions are made up of vessels of the Holy Spirit to carry out the assignments they have been given. Vessels of the Holy Spirit never argue with God over their assignments. There is no room for jealousy. Lives are at stake. When the bullets start flying, no one life is more important than another.

Perhaps it is time we learned that we need both hands and feet to be the body of Christ. We can't do without all our parts when we hit the battlefront. Suddenly, we're saying to one another, "If you don't do your job, I'm going to be hurt!" We'll be asking one another, "What do I need to do for you so that you can do your work better?" We'll be asking, "How can I pray for you?"

The time has come for the Church to move from personal misery to personal ministry. In fact, the cause of misery often defines that particular place of ministry. A person's mistakes can become his or her mission to others. The very mistakes that follow you, haunt you, torment you continuously can be used by God to help and to heal others. Inevitably, you are healed in the process of pouring out your life to meet someone else's needs.

The time has come for the Church to move from being a seeker of the Word to being a channel of the Word. That doesn't necessarily mean prophesying over people, though you can always edify, encourage and exhort others in spiritual thoughts and actions. A channel of God's Word identifies with the hurts, mistakes and misery of others to help them overcome their bondage. A channel of God's Word brings others to Christ and His Church as the Source of help.

This paradigm shift in perspective changes the reasons people go to the house of the Lord. Instead of coming to God's house seeking help, you come saying, "Who am I going to bless today? Who can I take with me? God, show me someone who needs ministry and love today." When hundreds of Christians in one congregation adopt this perspective and enlist in OPERATION HOMEFRONT, the rejoicing at the house of the Lord will raise the rafters. A local church will need to add more and more services to accommodate all the people.

Who exemplifies a vessel of the Holy Spirit?

> *Now there was one, Anna, a prophetess, the daughter of Phanuel, of the tribe of Asher. She was of a great age, and had lived with a husband seven years from her virginity; and this woman was a widow of about eighty-four years, who did not depart from the temple, but served God with fastings and prayers night and day. And coming in that instant, she gave thanks to the Lord, and spoke of Him to all those who looked for redemption in Jerusalem.* (Luke 2:36-38)

Notice how specific the text is in identifying this woman. If she had married at about 16 years old, as most Jewish girls did, and then lived with her husband for seven years, she was approximately 23 years old when she came to the temple to live.

Why did she come to the temple as a 23-year-old woman? She came in her misery. We don't know why her husband died, but this young woman was in terrible shape to have sought shelter in the temple. You can be sure that she did not come to the temple to become a prophetess. She came with a miserable, messed-up life, and she stayed to have her needs met.

But what did she turn out to be after praying and fasting, day and night, for apparently a long period of time. In the midst of misery and mistakes, God turned her life into ministry. Because she had prayed for many years, her eyes were clear. She recognized the Messiah. Then she began telling everyone that the redemption of Jerusalem was born!

I referred previously to the little handmaiden in Naaman's household who told her mistress that a prophet would heal her husband of his leprosy (2 Kings 5:1-4). Consider life from that handmaiden's perspective. She was a victim, taken captive. The Bible doesn't record what turmoil she had gone through, but I can assure you that she was miserable. She had lost her family, her nation, the practice of her religion, and her spiritual elders.

But God had strategically put her in the right place at the right time. The man who had captured her and destroyed her nation was her master. Do you know what most of us would have said about his leprosy? We'd say, "He deserves it! Let him die! God is judging him for warring against Israel!"

No! No! No! God's people must change their paradigm. This little girl was not bitter though she had every reason to be. I find that Christians who continually seek a Word from God or help for their problems have never learned to forgive and let go of offenses against them. But this handmaiden was a vessel that God could use.

She didn't even ask to be set free. She simply took advantage of the opportunity God had given to her. She pointed those who had put her in bondage to a solution for their problem. And what was the result? Naaman, the king, is healed. His words to the prophet say it all, "Indeed, now I know that there is no God in all the earth, except in Israel; now therefore, please take a gift from your servant" (2 Kings 5:15).

Get the message? Many unsung heroes throughout the Bible are used by God as His ground force. How did the great Apostle Peter hear about Jesus? His brother, Andrew, became a vessel of the Holy Spirit saying, "I want you to come see this man!" When the awards are given out at the end of the age, you're going to see Andrew standing there as tall as Peter.

What about the father that brought His epileptic son to Jesus? What about the centurion who came to Jesus concerning his servant? What about the mothers who brought their children to Jesus? You say, "They had needs to be met!" Yes, but they were vessels of the Holy Spirit for others—not just for themselves—although they received from Him, too.

Jesus called Matthew (Levi) from his job as a tax collector to follow Him. What is the first thing that Matthew does?

And he left all, rose up, and followed Him. Then Levi gave Him a great feast in his own house. And there were a great number of tax collectors and others who sat down with them. But their scribes and the Pharisees murmured against His disciples, saying, "Why do You eat and drink with tax collectors and sinners?" (Luke 5:28-30)

What a message! Matthew committed his life to Jesus, then he gathered all the people he had influence over to come to a banquet for Jesus. Matthew was a Door Keeper, a vessel of the Holy Spirit. He didn't spend the first year of following Jesus getting his problems solved and his needs met! He didn't corner

106

Jesus for personal counseling—he threw a party!

Too many Christians are trying to save themselves, or even save the world while they're losing their own families, communities and cities. Now is the time for vessels of the Holy Spirit to find their place in OPERATION HOMEFRONT. For me, that's Atlanta. For you, that's wherever you are, doing whatever you do.

Your opportunity is today. Don't wait! Don't look into the future! One day you will answer to God for the use of your life as a vessel.

If you're one called to the Prayer Watch, start praying. Take hold of the altar of God and don't let go for anything!

If you are a Ground Breaker, start plowing the ground so that the seed will take root. Let your life, your words and your songs prepare the ground, break it up for planting.

If you are a Door Keeper, stay on "go" for that opening, that opportunity, that moment to gain ground. When the door cracks, push it all the way open!

And if you are one of the Action Army, get busy! There's more to do than ever, but you'll find fulfillment and joy as never before.

The strongholds are broken. The enemy at home has been put to flight. God is empowering local churches around the world for a massive ground attack, boldly declaring His glory.

OPERATION HOMEFRONT! Forward! March!

6 The Church And The City

What is the greatest issue on planet Earth today? I'm sure you could list many serious problems: ecology, education, medical research, pornography, abortion, AIDS, drugs, the homeless. All of these are major issues that overshadow the quality of living for everyone in our society, and all of these deserve attention. But a far greater issue affecting the quality of life on this planet is the relationship between the Church and the city.

No other people on earth have the opportunity of changing the ills of our world more than responsible Christians. God has called, chosen, instructed and empowered His people to fill the earth with Kingdom authority. That does not mean a "takeover," but it certainly does mean a saturation of every facet of life with the message and demonstration of righteousness, peace and joy in the Holy Spirit.

Two thousand years ago Jesus rode triumphantly into the city of Jerusalem.

> *Then the multitudes who went before and those who followed cried out, saying: "Hosanna to the Son of David! 'Blessed is He who comes in the name of the Lord!' Hosanna in the highest!" And when He had come into Jerusalem, all the city was moved, saying, "Who is this?" So the multitudes said, "This is Jesus, the prophet from Nazareth of Galilee." Then Jesus went into the temple of God, and drove out all those who bought and sold in the temple, and overturned the tables of the moneychangers and the seats of those who sold doves. And He said to them, "It is written, 'My house shall be called a house of prayer,' but you have made it a 'den of thieves.' " Then the blind and the lame came to Him in the temple, and He healed them. But when the chief priests and scribes saw the wonderful things that He did, and the children crying out in the temple and saying, "Hosanna to the Son of David!" they were indignant and said to Him, "Do You hear what these are saying?" And Jesus said to them, "Yes. Have you never read, 'Out of the mouth of babes and nursing infants You have perfected praise'?" (Matthew 21:9-16)*

Jesus' first action after a triumphant entry into the city of Jerusalem was to go directly to the temple and address the corrup-

110

tion He found there. Jesus had cried over the city of Jerusalem, knowing that the key to solving their problems rested in the true purposes of the temple. Jerusalem was a city under great oppression, and Jesus wept because the people would not hear the prophetic voice.

Jesus had walked throughout Galilee teaching principles of quality living. He had opened doors for people to become free and whole. His entire ministry culminated in that victorious entry into Jerusalem, because He had focused continually upon describing a Kingdom authority unlike the governments of this world. Seemingly, he had won the popular election by this display of support and acceptance.

At the time Jerusalem was a city struggling under the weight of political oppression, financial strain, religious anarchy, insurrections and the plotting of subversive groups. In the midst of these conditions, Jesus calls for the disciples to bring Him a colt to ride into the city. He mounts an unbroken, untrained colt and rides amid the rot of that society as a prophetic sign to them— and to us today!

Jesus rides into the middle of the city triumphantly, and then He goes immediately to the very heart of the problem. He does not go to City Hall, the schools, the business districts or medical research laboratories. He goes to the temple. He wants all the citizens cheering Him on to know where the center of their city's well-being really resides. Jesus wants them to know that when the temple is cleansed, the rest of the city will begin to recover.

Whenever the Church has lost its morals, its power and its purpose, the city and the communities throughout its region suffer the consequences. The reverse is also true. Whenever the Church and Christians individually awaken themselves to address the problems of their communities, life throughout a city rejuvenates. The entire atmosphere changes from decay into positive action and energy.

Martin Luther's act of nailing 95 Theses on the door of Wittenberg Cathedral in Germany in 1915 demonstrates the path to solutions. That one act by a courageous man triggered the Reformation. Out of the Reformation the Renaissance emerges, releasing the creativity and productivity in people to change cities and nations. Art flourished. Music filled the air. People began to dream and create and invent answers to the plagues that oppressed them.

An alive Church is God's solution to the devastation of our cities. But instead of the Church marching boldly in the streets of our cities to give solutions, God's people hide in the suburbs. We have been strangled, mocked by the media and ignored by politicians. God is saying one more time, "Let's see if they will act; let's see if people will hear."

The blatant de-emphasis of the Church's influence in society is clearly reflected in city life today. Jesus never once separated problems of any nature from the prevailing spiritual climate— individually or corporately. Jesus called out the names of specific cities for judgment because they refused to hear the prophetic word delivered to them.

Jesus rebuked the city of Capernaum.

> *"And you, Capernaum, who are exalted to heaven, will be brought down to Hades; for if the mighty works which were done in you had been done in Sodom [notice, another city], it would have remained until this day. But I say to you that it shall*

be more tolerable for the land of Sodom in the day of judgment than for you." (Matthew 11:23,24)

Notice that Sodom fell because of moral problems—not lack of government funding or of brilliant leadership. Sodom was destroyed because of the perverse spiritual climate of that city. God will judge cities individually for their receptivity to ministry.

Jesus addressed the spiritual climate of other cities:

"Woe to you, Chorazin! Woe to you, Bethsaida! For if the mighty works which were done in you had been done in Tyre and Sidon, they would have repented long ago in sackcloth and ashes. But I say to you, it will be more tolerable for Tyre and Sidon in the day of judgment than for you." (Matthew 11:21,22)

What have you just read? Jesus says to us that our cities are in disarray because of the lack of spiritual receptivity. Where is God's voice? Where is prophetic leadership? Why are Spirit-filled men and women silent when they hold the well-being of their cities in the balance?

Think about the patterns of cities in productivity and cities in devastation that we learn from history. You can see the correlation between historical periods of devastation and the front page headlines of our newspapers today to understand what the causes of problems in the inner city really are. Whenever God's people are silent, tyranny reigns.

In every historical period of great upheaval and oppression, the Church has sat silently by. What is the Church doing today to address the devastation of our cities? Why do we appear to be so ineffective in addressing the root problems of our communities with workable solutions?

One reason! The Church is fragmented and confused about her identity. The majority of Christians don't even know who they are in shaping the atmosphere and the events in their own neighborhoods—much less in world events. Christians don't feel as if they can change anything, or that they should get involved. Church activities are regarded as the "do-good" preoccupations of nice people that won't matter much in the long run. We spend more time on church dinners and socials than on social action.

Recently I talked with a group of people in my office who told me that the city fathers did not want any churches in Atlanta to be involved in hosting international guests during the 1996 Olympics. This group informed me that major churches in our city with thousands of members should leave plans for any input or visibility of a religious nature to a small parachurch group. In other words, Atlanta's spiritual fathers should sit still and keep their mouths shut during the Olympics in our city.

Am I surprised? No! Should I abide by that request? Not without a confrontation on the matter! The Church leaders in a city have been relegated to the "back of the bus" long enough. I also intend to initiate some dialogue about the state lottery that Georgia's newly-elected governor advocates as a source of finances designated for education. I not only oppose instituting a lottery, but I am also convinced that the funds do not benefit education or anything else in the long run. The negative effects of a lottery upon a community far outweigh any temporary benefits of the initial additional revenue.

The authority of the Church is constantly de-emphasized in the courts. The idea of separating church and state as the concept is interpreted and enforced today totally disregards the provisions of that concept as it was proposed by our founding Fathers. The writers of our Constitution intended to protect the freedom of religious expression. They wanted to ensure that no one was bound by a corrupt religious system. They never intended to limit the practice of people's beliefs, but only to protect them. Separating church and state in the decision-making over a city will ensure a city's slow, painful destruction.

In the spirit of rebellion against God's supremacy, many government leaders ignore God's resources. They place themselves on thrones of authority. For example, some decisions of the Supreme Court in recent years mock the very existence of God. Moral violations protected under the law imply that the government sees itself as God. Meanwhile, we pay homage to the government. We give it our money. We look to it for safety and provisions. We honor its mandates as the right things to think and to believe.

And what are the results of worshipping a false god? The results are always destructive—a world without form and void. False gods close off provisions and resources so that people are left in despair. God's judgment falls upon those following false gods. In the process, people always suffer and die, then communities die, then cities die. The wage of sin is always death.

So what is the dilemma of the Church in this regard? Do we remain silent and still? Do we ignore people's cries for help? Is it even possible to reverse some of the destructive patterns that our society has adopted with such disregard for what is right and true?

At the end of the depression in the '40s, many changes occurred in society that spelled the end of the strong influence of local churches. Mothers began working more and more to provide a heightened standard of living for their families. Divorce increased. Inevitably, traditional family roles and expectations changed drastically. Ethnic cultural distinctions began to diminish with an influx of immigrants into the U.S.

Society's values changed. Education became much more factual than moral in its content. People began focusing more on job skills and practical matters than on intrinsic rewards found in art, literature and music. The computer age revolutionized the job market.

Our life-styles changed. Preserving the environment has in recent decades become a major issue of survival. The family has been redefined. The workplace has become more like home than the house where family members live together. And as a result of all these factors, cities face tremendous obstacles. Economic polarization has imprisoned many people in an urban nightmare with no way out.

But there are solutions, and I pray that it isn't too late! Jesus cried out, "Jerusalem, Jerusalem . . . ," but no one responded. Today few voices are even crying out! Unless a prophetic cry pierces the night, our nation is headed for a collision between the "haves" and the "have nots." Inevitably, we will face the consequences of an economic civil upheaval.

But there is hope. People today are longing for that sense of community and close relationship that ensures health and safety. The wave of patriotism and nostalgia that is currently sweeping our nation indicates the desire for a return to solid values. It's interesting that among the least visible of those old-fashioned, refurbished institutions is the Church. Where is the visible Church?

A recent religious survey conducted by the Graduate School of the City University of New York revealed that the U.S. is broadly religious and widely diverse. The study—the most comprehensive effort to draw a portrait of religion in America—found that 90% of Americans identify with a religion. The survey found that 86.5 percent of Americans (214 million) consider themselves to be Christians. So where are they? ("90% of Americans Identify With a Religion," *The Atlanta Journal and Constitution*, April 10, 1991, p. A1.)

The current desire for commitment is essential to a mighty spiritual revival worldwide, which rumbles now in the beginning stages. But before the influx of millions of people returning to churches reaches major proportions, the Church must address many flaws of its own. Internal battles still rage. The Church lacks unity and a common cause, a common voice. Many people still view the Church as a place for spiritual nurturing and salvation, while the domestic and political issues of life are left to the direction of social experts.

The potential impact that the Church could have upon cities awaits our getting our own house in order. Until we do, people will look for answers outside the doors of the Church. They will continue to maintain a form of godliness—belief in God—without committing themselves to any place of prayer, communion and growth that is central to spiritual well-being and effective Christian service.

St. Augustine said, "No salvation exists outside the church." Martin Luther, the great reformer, said, "Outside this Christian church, there is no salvation or forgiveness of sin, but only everlasting death and damnation." And Jesus said, "Blessed are you, Simon Barjonah, for flesh and blood has not revealed this to you, but My Father who is in heaven. And I say to you, Peter, that on this rock [the revelation I have given you] I will build My church, and the gates of hell will not prevail against it." The only authority to act in God's name is within His Church.

Only the Church has the right to say, "Hell, no!" Not government. Not society. Not education. Only the Church has been granted the keys to lock up evil forces or to unlock heavenly resources for the benefit of society. Do I believe we are doing that today? To some extent, but not anywhere near the dimension God will grant to us whenever people who know God and believe in God are willing to pay the price for that kind of authority.

A major problem in local churches around the world today is the lack of spiritual leadership. God has allowed a maintenance program to exist until a generation of bold, willing leaders will step forward and declare that He is Lord. We only enter the sheepfold through the door that is Jesus Christ Himself. Jesus has called shepherds to tend His sheep. Too many shepherds today are more concerned about their own plans and maintaining boundaries than they are in fulfilling God's purposes for that sheepfold in their city.

WHAT JESUS INTENDS FOR HIS CHURCH TO DO

What does Jesus intend for His Church to be like as we approach the 21st Century? First of all, **we are to challenge the gates of hell**. The first thing people associate with "hell" is anger—as in "mad as hell." We are to challenge anything that attacks truth, righteousness, peace and goodness. We must take a stand against any vicious, destructive forces destroying our communities.

Jesus intends for His Church to restore city life to a positive, productive, safe environment. Jesus' first sermon was that He came to preach to the poor. Today Jesus would march directly into the streets of our cities where poverty and homelessness breed to address the conditions there. The Church sits idly by without solutions when the first item on Jesus' ministry agenda was to preach to the poor.

And what was Jesus' message to poor people? He told them how to tap their inner resources to get out of poverty. He told them about spiritual riches. He assured them that when spiritual treasures are the focus of their lives on earth, material needs are met.

Instead of addressing poverty, many Christians move into the suburbs and build high walls around their homes. They do not believe Jesus is a solution to poverty. They are afraid to invest themselves in helping others out of a ditch. They run from the challenge of breaking the poverty cycle in public housing by risking to reach out a hand of love.

Jesus intends for His Church to heal people's broken hearts. Who are the brokenhearted? Open your eyes. The broken-hearted are children whose lives are shattered by divorce. They are lonely, elderly people who have lost all purpose in life. They are people who are sick with AIDS or addicted to cocaine. They are people who are well dressed, well educated, driving fancy cars and living in huge houses who think about suicide constantly. Jesus said for His Church to heal their broken hearts.

Jesus intends for His Church to redeem cities from the grip of evil forces that are smothering and choking the life out of

that city. The Church represents freedom from captivity. I ministered recently, as I have numerous times through the years, at the Union Mission in downtown Atlanta. I was struck by the hopelessness in the faces of those people as I spoke with them. Life had been choked out of them, and many couldn't even look into my eyes as I spoke. They were beaten down by life. So what is the answer?

Jesus intends for His Church to open the eyes of the blind to see their potential and their value to Him. People need to see themselves as God sees them. They can see when we open their eyes through our own love and compassion toward their hurts and their disappointments. Our love can heal their blindness.

Jesus intends for His Church to set at liberty those who are oppressed. What oppresses them? Their weaknesses, their failures, their mistakes. Many addicted to drugs cannot bear to face the reality of their lives. They need to know about forgiveness through Christ, Who gives them a new beginning. They need the power of the Holy Spirit to set them free from all kinds of spiritual bondages.

Jesus intends for His Church to challenge the gates of hell, to proclaim the gospel of the Kingdom and to destroy the works of the devil. We live and move as an army at war against evil. At the same time we are creating community relationships that will arm us against all the strategy of the enemy to stop us. We are enjoying the benefits of abundant living and choosing God's standards for our households. We fight with both offensive and defensive weapons in waging war.

The demonstration that God is raising up to restore cities is something we have lost. I went to a private home in such a community recently, and on my way there I saw a man in a little boat fishing in a pond near his house at about 9:00 p.m. I thought to myself, "Is it possible that we could turn around the tide of fear that keeps most people isolated from one another? Is it still possible to feel safe outdoors in your community after dark? Is it possible for people to discover a way of life more valuable to them than watching television, or running to a fancy restaurant, or going to the theater?"

Only Jesus' Church holds the keys to salvation. We have been entrusted with taking the good news of reconciliation between God and man to every living creature. Only Jesus' Church has been entrusted with the right to forgive sins. We can hear the confessions of others and grant them absolution through the blood of Jesus Christ. Only Jesus' Church is a storehouse of healing, resources and direction to anyone who needs something from God.

Only Jesus' Church dispenses His sacraments to heal and maintain people in this world through His eternal covenants. Observing the sacraments is not optional for Christians. The Church administers grace and forgiveness in a continual renewal process that makes imperfect, fallible people qualify for an extraordinary mission. The sacraments make us to be worthy vessels for the Lord's use.

God gave me a dream one night years ago that revolutionized my ministry. Since that time, the one message God has put into my mouth is about the Kingdom of God. I have been called a heretic, a false prophet and a cult teacher because of that message, but the Kingdom of God was the only message that Jesus ever preached. For several years, all my energy in ministry was directed toward communicating that message.

My attempts to communicate an understanding of the Kingdom of God included writing books, going on television, meeting with other teachers whom God had spoken to about His Kingdom such as Ern Baxter, Bob Mumford, T.L. Osborne and others. I sent ministry teams to numerous third world nations. I will not speculate on the scope of my influence in getting that message out, but I will say that I am amazed and grateful to God for so many open doors. The extent of that message has literally gone around the world.

Now God has placed me in a posture of Kingdom demonstration that is the focus of my ministry today. A complete witness includes both communication and demonstration. One without the other lacks effectiveness in bringing about change. The dream I related to you in chapter one of this book has created the impetus for the remainder of my ministry. What did that dream say to me?

First of all, **cities lack spiritual leadership**. I continued throughout the dream searching for my Presbytery, and I believe that signifies absent leaders in the Church generally. Anything that separates leaders from local churches will destroy their ministries. God's authority to influence the world resides and flows from local churches into communities and cities.

God only wrote to the local churches in Asia in the Revelation of Jesus Christ. He instructed John to record what he saw, and send out His messages to local churches. They needed the Revelation of Jesus to reveal Him to the unsaved world.

Ministries that operate outside of the covering and relationship to local churches are making a grave mistake. God will not bless ministries that come into a city, get a mailing list of Christians from churches all over that city and then hit them every month for financial support. I don't care whether this applies to a prophet, or an apostle or a traveling ministry. If they separate themselves from local churches and do not recognize the spiritual leaders of that city, their ministries will die.

Imagine what would happen if every local church in a city came alive and realized that they were a deposit of God and spoke as one voice to that city! They would determine which candidates were elected. Wouldn't it be marvelous if the church would rise up and say, "Hold it a minute. You have laughed at the church, and now we are going to show you that you can't override the morals of the Christian community. We don't want a lottery in this state, and we don't want our children to be educated with funds raised from gambling."

Don't tell me we can't do it! Are we afraid to speak out? Are we afraid of prison? I can still hear Daddy King's voice in my mind saying to us during the Civil Rights movement, "Boys, are you willing to go to jail for this?" If the Church is truly alive, the answer is "Yes!"

WHAT WILL SAVE OUR CITIES?

Only the Church has the authority to bind and loose spiritual forces and to determine the moral decisions of people. I am reminded of President Bush's question to me about how our church was able to bring blacks and whites together in racial harmony. I answered, "Sir, it is because of the Spirit of God."

Problems in society are never solved by might, power, or the strength of committees or organizations. The true answers to life's most perplexing problems are found in the work of the Holy Spirit within people's hearts. What does that mean specifically—in terms of what we are to do?

1. **The Church must march into the city.** This "march" calls for bold action. We need to ask for meetings with our city leaders and voice our views. We need to lobby or picket if necessary to oppose unjust laws. We need to grant—and even request—interviews with the press to express our opinions. We need to offer help, solutions and alternatives to every problem we address. It's not enough to simply complain; we must offer answers.

2. **The Church must assume its role as the only custodian of God's grace.** The purposes of the local church grant it the right to affect the lives of those living in the community where it is located. It is the church that dedicates babies, buries the dead, marries people, counsels the lonely and brokenhearted, administers the Lord's Table and Baptism, and so on. The members of that local church are the body of Christ to that community. They have every right to assume the role of custodians for the well-being of people living around them.

We must not become intimidated about living out our identities as caring, protective citizens with a plan for making conditions better. We cannot afford to think, "It's none of my business" whenever we see places ruled by destructive forces. We must gain confidence in realizing that we are God's voice in that situation. The true Church of Jesus Christ must stand up and know who she is.

3. **The Church must initiate a renewed emphasis on the spiritual needs of people.** People are composed of bodies, souls and spirits. For the past forty years, the emphasis in society has focused upon meeting the physical, emotional and intellectual needs of people, but the spiritual aspects of human needs have

been distorted or ignored. This omission is especially notable in the curriculum of our schools. I believe that this lack of recognizing the spiritual dimension of human beings is one of the major reasons that education is in such crisis today.

The needs and fears of people transcend this natural plane. The spiritual condition of a person will determine the quality of every relationship, every goal and every decision that person makes throughout life. When the Church brings people to a recognition of their spiritual needs, many of the root problems of our society will be resolved.

4. **The Church must assume the responsibility of ending the cycle of poverty.** How do we do that? Two ways. First of all, we must preach to poverty. Preach what? Poor people need to know the principle of giving to others. People prosper from God whenever they give. People with a "get" mentality will always remain in bondage to their unmet needs. The principle of sowing and reaping will work for anyone. If you sow seed, you reap a harvest. That law is not speculation; it will always work.

Secondly, we must educate the children of low income families. Their reading skills need to be of primary importance to citizens of any city. Education is a ticket out of poverty. An education is necessary to gain the professional proficiency that will break the generational poverty cycle. If government dollars are going anywhere to remedy the problems of cities, this is where they need to be spent.

Poverty breeds poverty. I would very much like to do away with public housing altogether. Are we going to throw away those families? No! We need to give them something better to do. We need to concentrate our efforts on giving incentives and stimulating motivation to break the cycle. Handouts destroy self-esteem. We need to do everything we can to open new avenues of life to people living in public housing in the inner city.

5. **The Church must give support to any cause, project or program that strengthens family life.** Government subsidy programs need to help families stay together. We must become vocal in advocating any policies that reward families and penalize broken homes—everything from tax breaks to financial aid. We need to be bold in helping couples who are hanging in there with one another. The Church must work to change the mentality of Americans concerning the family and family values.

Some social scientists are predicting that by the year 2000, 80% of American women will be in the workplace. Who is taking care of their children? Providing child care is an excellent way for the Church to influence a nation. Those working mothers would not only have the benefit of leaving their children with positive, trustworthy role models, but they would also reap the benefits of godly principles being instilled into the minds of those children from an early age. That strategy alone could turn our nation around.

6. **The Church must promote quality living in the inner city.** That translates into quality facilities and quality leadership. The inner city must provide a safe, clean environment if it is to challenge the list of benefits that cause people to move to the suburbs. Currently, all the options in daily living are accessible in the suburbs, but not in the inner city. "Quality living" must be the central purpose of strong bonds between the work of government leaders and of church leaders.

7. **The Church must promote the concept of community living.** We need to know our neighbors. We need to know the people who live around us as well as the ones we work with or

socialize with. A word that Christians often use in our vernacular describes the foundations of a community spirit. That word is "fellowship." Fellowship implies caring and relating in a way that people really know one another.

> *". . . If we walk in the light as He is in the light, we have fellowship with one another, and the blood of Jesus Christ His Son cleanses us from all sin."* (1 John 1:7)

Fellowship is community. True fellowship is the Kingdom of God, and that comes by involvement, not just by observation. It takes the commitment of many to make a community, but the effort is worth it. Who better than the Church can demonstrate to all the love and the fellowship of true community. Jesus said they would recognize those who belong to Him by their love. And in that demonstration, we will tap the heartfelt desires of millions of people who are longing for a sense of acceptance, productivity and wholeness.

Can our cities by saved? Adopting public housing communities and taking our love and our skills directly to those needing help is one answer. Caring, committed people become the new role models of children in those communities, replacing the drug lords.

Until the hope for realizing one's potential filters into every community in every city, into every household, into the minds and hearts of every member of every family regardless of their race, economics, sex or age, the Church cannot rest. The stakes are too high. The steeples towering over our cities represent the solutions to the problems. Before the 21st Century, we have the potential of solving racial, economic and political problems that

can set standards to be duplicated around the world. Will we?
Can we? We must!

7 Fires
Of Passion

My mother, Addie Mae Tomberlin Paulk, died in April of this year at age 83. For several weeks Mama had become increasingly unresponsive to things going on around her. When I received a call that her condition was seemingly worse, I told my nephew and his wife to take Mama to the hospital emergency room, and I would meet them there.

When I saw Mama at the hospital, she didn't respond to my voice, which was most unusual. She wouldn't open her eyes. Her limbs hung totally lifeless. In my mind flashed the thought of a message I had given to the teenagers of our church about the spirit of death oppressing their generation. Suddenly, the Spirit of the Lord spoke to me, "This is the way the Church is, too. None of the parts of the body work. The eyes don't see. The ears don't hear."

Ezekiel prophesied over dead, dry bones, and the bones came together. Out of dry bones, God breathed life into them and created a great army. How do we bring life into the bones of the Church?

In those days John the Baptist came preaching in the wilderness of Judea, and saying, "Repent, for the kingdom of heaven is at hand!" For this is he who was spoken of by the prophet Isaiah, saying, "The voice of one crying in the wilderness: 'Prepare the way of the Lord; Make His paths straight.' " Now John himself was clothed in camel's hair, with a leather belt around his waist; and his food was locusts and wild honey. Then Jerusalem, all Judea, and all the region around the Jordan went out to him and were baptized by him in the Jordan, confessing their sins.

But when he saw many of the Pharisees and Sadducees coming to his baptism, he said to them, "Brood of vipers! Who warned you to flee from the wrath to come? Therefore bear fruits worthy of repentance, and do not think to say to yourselves, 'We have Abraham as our father.' For I say to you that God is able to raise up children to Abraham from these stones. And even now the ax is laid to the root of the trees.

"Therefore every tree which does not bear good fruit is cut down and thrown into the fire. I indeed baptize

you with water unto repentance, but He who is com-
ing after me is mightier than I, whose sandals I am
not worthy to carry. He will baptize you with the Holy
Spirit and fire." (Matthew 3:1-12)

"The Holy Spirit and fire!" Since I was a very young child, I've been hearing those words. In almost every reference, the writer or speaker associated "fire" with purging—which is truly one aspect of God's fire. But the purposes of "fire" certainly are not limited to purging. References to "fire" in the Bible include a variety of connotations for the word.

For example, we are told that "God is a consuming fire" (Hebrews 12:29). Certainly, that description does not refer to purging. Fire is a source of power and the release of great energy. If that is true, and Jesus is to baptize the body of Christ with the Holy Spirit and fire, why is the body of Christ so lifeless and unresponsive to the Lord? I began in my own mind to ask that question while exploring the meaning and purpose of fire.

The sun is 93 million miles away from the earth. The sun is a consuming fire, much like the burning bush that Moses saw in the wilderness. Because the fire of the sun burns continually 93 million miles away, life flourishes on this planet. The sun provides warmth, energy, and it is a significant factor in creating the atmospheric conditions necessary to sustain and perpetuate continual vegetation and animal life cycles.

And how is the word "fire" used throughout Scripture?

From the brightness before Him, His thick clouds
passed with hailstones and coals of fire. The Lord
thundered from heaven, and the Most High uttered
His voice, hailstones and coals of fire. He sent out His

*arrows and scattered the foe, lightnings in abun-
dance, and He vanquished them. Then the channels
of the sea were seen, the foundations of the world
were uncovered at Your rebuke, O Lord, at the blast
of the breath of Your nostrils.* (Psalm 18:12-15)

Notice the words "blast," "thunder" and "fire" to describe
God's awesome power to rebuke. Fire is often used in describing man's interaction with a holy God. Paul speaks about the
coming of the Lord by saying that He will destroy "the lawless
one" with fire (2 Thessalonians 1:8). Fire both precedes and
follows the biblical accounts of Jesus' second coming.

Of course, the Holy Spirit is always associated with fire—even
as a spoken title, "the Holy Spirit and fire." We hear that said so
often that we miss both the truth and the expectation of what
the identity of the Holy Spirit's fire represents. We who are filled
with the Holy Spirit are also, presumably, filled with fire to
empower us as ministers unto God.

*. . . Who makes His angels spirits, His ministers a
flame of fire.* (Psalm 104:4; Hebrews 1:7)

Often the Word of the Lord itself is also associated with fire.
Certainly the Word coming from the mouth of God or Jesus'
voice in the judgment is associated with fire. God asks,

*"Is not My word like a fire?" says the Lord, "And like
a hammer that breaks the rock into pieces?"*
(Jeremiah 23:29)

As I began contemplating the Word of God in relation to fire, I
was struck with what seems to be a paradox. The Holy Spirit can

132

dwell in someone who does not experience or even give evidence of the presence of God's fire in his or her life. I began to understand a deeper meaning of "quenching the Holy Spirit." The life of a Christian can be spiritually dead and lifeless any time the Holy Spirit is ignored or not given full reign. That explains the reason that Spirit-filled people can live without any anointing upon their lives.

What is the work of the Holy Spirit's fire within your life? The Holy Spirit guides, teaches and directs. The Holy Spirit empowers your witness. The Holy Spirit brings clarity to the purposes of God for your life within your mind and heart. The Holy Spirit within you responds to any word or anointing from God in someone else's life to bring you into spiritual unity with that person.

But you control the degree of that response! I have stood in amazement at the lack of response in teenagers today toward the same ministry that would have brought the house down no more than eight years ago. Many times I will hear an anointed song during the services at Chapel Hill Harvester Church, and I'll think, "If that song had been sung at the camp meetings I attended as a boy, they would have sung it for thirty minutes or more." Meanwhile, I see little response in some of the faces in my own congregation, and I ask, "Why, God?"

The body is lifeless. Just because a church teaches about the Holy Spirit, that church doesn't necessarily burn with the fire of the Holy Spirit. Oh, He is present among the people every time they come together! But if He has very little receptivity or reign within them, that gathering is lifeless. But what happens when the fire is present?

Then one of the seraphim flew to me, having in his hand a live coal which he had taken with the tongs from the altar. And he touched my mouth with it, and said: "Behold, this has touched your lips; Your iniquity is taken away, And your sin purged." Also I heard the voice of the Lord saying: "Whom shall I send, and who will go for Us?" Then I said, "Here am I! Send me." (Isaiah 6:6-8)

I believe we live in a day when God is taking the coal of fire from the altar and touching the lips of those whose hearts are receptive to His commands. God is touching both their lips and their lives. Not only are the sins of these messengers purged, but God is challenging them with assignments from His throne.

When this experience is genuine, the only response possible is, "Here am I! Send me." I sense such a deep desire in so many people today to be released to do the ministry God has equipped them to do. Perhaps those talents and skills have sat on the shelf collecting dust for many years. No matter! This is the time that God is saying, "Who will go?"

This kind of experience cannot be separated from the Upper Room happening of Pentecost. Like the coals of fire from God's altar that touched Isaiah's mouth, 120 people sat expectantly, in total agreement with one another in an Upper Room in Jerusalem. Suddenly, fires of the Holy Spirit looking like tongues sat upon the heads of those believers.

So what is this "Holy Spirit and fire" that John the Baptist promised us Jesus would bring? It is the same coals of fire that touched Isaiah's mouth and the tongues of fire that danced on the heads of those 120 gathered at Pentecost! If that sounds exciting, it certainly is! But having the fire of God's anointing will also bring great tribulation.

> *O Lord, You induced me, and I was persuaded; You are stronger than I, and have prevailed. I am in derision daily; everyone mocks me. For when I spoke, I cried out; I shouted, "Violence and plunder!" Because the word of the Lord was made to me a reproach and a derision daily. Then I said, "I will not make mention of Him, nor speak anymore in His name." But His word was in my heart like a burning fire shut up in my bones; I was weary of holding it back, and I could not. For I heard many mocking: "Fear on every side!" "Report," they say, "and we will report it!" All my acquaintances watched for my stumbling, saying, "Perhaps he can be induced; then we will prevail against him, and we will take revenge on him." But the Lord is with me as a mighty, awesome One. Therefore my persecutors will stumble, and will not prevail. They will be greatly ashamed, for they will not prosper. Their everlasting confusion will never be forgotten.* (Jeremiah 20:7-11)

Jeremiah's assignment from God was to preach against the corruption of cities. The prophet warned the people that their cities were going to be destroyed. The King sent for Jeremiah and threatened to stop his preaching of that message. The officials not only put the prophet in prison, but they also put him in a miry pit and almost suffocated him.

In Jeremiah 28, even the priests warned Jeremiah to tone down his sermons and prophesy some new material. I'm sure they were telling Jeremiah to talk about the new buildings or the positive steps the government was taking in that city instead of warning people of coming disaster. They would advise Jeremiah to tell the truth on a different subject that would make everyone look good.

No wonder Jeremiah decided not to proclaim the word of the Lord anymore (verse 9). I talk with numerous parents, business-people and even pastors who feel the same way. The fires of God upon your life will always bring this kind of pressure from people around you. They will not want to hear what God is really saying—especially if they are being warned about impending danger.

Some of the most fired-up Christians I've ever met have been at this same place in ministry. They have wanted to quit. They've cried out to God, "God, I can't take it anymore! I've said what You told me to say; I've shouted Your solutions as loud as I possibly can; I've pleaded with people to hear—but I'm at the end! I just can't go on! People hate me for being true to Your word!" But what happens? His Word is like fire in their bones!

I believe that God wants every Christian's mouth to be touched by tongs carrying flaming coals. I believe that God wants every Christian to know the surge of His Spirit that produces tongues of fire upon their heads. I believe that God intends for every Christian to feel fire shut up in his or her bones that leaves us no choice but to speak and act as a witness for God.

I have been preaching "the Holy Spirit and fire" longer than most Christians have been alive, yet I'm seeing something new and exciting about God's fire today that I know is significant for us to understand. Many Pentecostal denominations have become still, cold corpses because they have allowed God's fire to go out. In many Charismatic services you will find a cheer-leader at the front trying to pull worship out of people. They flash the words of one chorus after another upon the wall think-ing, "Maybe this will do it!"

What is missing? No one has touched their mouths with coals from God's altars. The only solutions to life are found in the fire of the Holy Spirit. So I began a diligent scriptural study of the word "fire." I looked up the word in Greek and in Hebrew. The best definition I could find for this "fire" of the Spirit is the word "passion."

Jesus saw the multitudes, and He was moved with "compas-sion." The fire of God was a reality to Jesus as He walked the paths of Galilee on a mission from God. He knew the reality of "fire in His bones" to say whatever the Father told Him to say. When He saw people scattered and confused, He felt the fire of God rise within Him.

Look carefully at this little group of disciples before they were consumed by fire at Pentecost. They argued for position—sitting at the right or left of Jesus' throne. Their treasurer was a thief. They lacked the power to cast out devils. Repeatedly, they lacked the faith to carry out instructions that Jesus gave them. They didn't understand Jesus' words—even after He explained them. One among them would deny Jesus, and another would betray Him. At the cross, they all ran away in fear except for John.

After three years of concentrated ministry, Jesus was crucified and was raised from the dead. The Bible says that He taught them for forty days about the Kingdom of God after His resur-rection (Acts 1:3). Even at His ascension, the disciples still did not understand what Jesus had taught them. They asked Him,

"Lord, will You at this time restore the kingdom to Israel?" (Acts 1:6).

I wouldn't blame Jesus for thinking, "My God! I've invested all this time in you, and you still don't understand what this is all about? How long do I have to put up with your carnal minds? You're still wondering what you will get out of this!"

This scene gives insight into the reason Jesus knew Peter didn't come up with answers about Jesus' identity as "the Christ, the Son of the living God" on his own. But Jesus patiently says to this lifeless group, easily filled with fear and constantly warring among themselves, ". . . but tarry in the city of Jerusalem until you are endued with power from on high" (Luke 24:49).

This "power from on high" is the fire, the passion of God. The fires of passion revolutionized those disciples. They sprung into action. Filled with fire, they could believe God could do anything through them! The fire in their bones could not be quenched— even at the threat of death! For the first time, those disciples knew the intensity and drive of fire that had directed Jesus every day. For the first time, they understood the things He said! For the first time, they had the faith to do the things He did!

What drives a spaceship beyond gravity into our solar system? Fire. What is the energy that moves your car? Fire. A car sits motionless until someone turns on the "ignition" to burn fuel. The fire of God sends us forth to accomplish great things for God. That fire burns as a passion to know and serve the Lord that can resist all kinds of "gravity" that pull us down to earth.

People—good Christians—can know the Lord's love and salvation and never understand the revolutionizing dimension of

His passion. The witness of the Holy Spirit within someone can motivate them merely to the level of asking God what He can do for them now! These Christians sing to get goose pimples. They go to meeting after meeting seeking a word from God. They may talk constantly of the "Holy Spirit" at work in their lives, but they have missed His fire that will turn the world upside down!

The 120 gathered in the Upper Room in obedience to Jesus' instructions were there to receive something from God. The Holy Spirit filled that room as a mighty rushing wind. Tongues of fire leaped above their heads. Those people came down the steps of that Upper Room so ignited by the fire of God that they couldn't think of one single thing to ask God to give them. Their eyes burned with passion.

The Revelation of Jesus Christ given to John describes Jesus' eyes as burning like a flame of fire (Revelation 1:14). That is the response Christ is awaiting in the eyes of His bride—a fire of passion for the things of God. The alternative is a lifeless body, unmoved against devastation. Devastation where? Devastation of what? Your family. Your church. Your community. Your schools. Your city. Your nation. But when your life catches fire for God, your greatest desire becomes, "God! Release me to do something for you! Here am I! Send me!"

The fire of God will ignite your imagination and your creativity. New ideas will flood your mind. The Holy Spirit can light a fire in the bones of your business. It will rekindle your marriage. It will get you off the golf courses and lakes and tennis courts (where I go) to put that energy into something productive for God. God's fire makes you action-oriented.

The fire of God leads many volunteers from Chapel Hill Harvester Church into Bankhead Courts, an Atlanta public housing community, on a weekly basis to offer reading programs, classes on building self-esteem, sports programs, arts programs, and other activities. The fire of God draws many medical professionals in our church to seek out the homeless in Atlanta's inner city and minister to them. The fire of God leads many of our ministerial staff to hospitals every week to minister to people who have AIDS. Why? The passion of God burns in their bones.

Atlanta, like every city in America, needs people with God's fire within them to get involved and make a difference. We don't need platitudes. We don't need religious people who want to tell everyone how bad they are without offering alternatives. We need people with fire who know how to march onto the devil's turf and wage a spiritual war. Some bears and wolves out there devouring our cities need some sharp-shooters to resist their fiery darts with the fire of God.

Some Christians see themselves as "little lambs that are slain." No, Jesus is the Lamb that was slain. He rose out of the grave and gave His Church authority, power and a commission to go. A passive, inactive Christian is a misnomer. People with a passion for God cannot keep from going, doing, living life fully. Passion is a consuming fire, a consuming force that demands action.

Passion can best be understood in the negative—which is so common—because we believe people with positive passion to be exceptions. Paul writes the church at Rome about men burning for men and women burning for women from passions that are aberrated. Paul said that they "burned in their lust for one another" (Romans 1:27). Paul writes concerning marriage, ". . . it is better to marry than to burn with passion" (1 Corinthians

7:9).

This is the same response in the negative of the passionate motivation that we need to have toward God. True passion will not turn you loose. This passion wakes you up every morning. This passion burns as you get into bed at night. Every part of your being burns. The tongue is like a little fire (James 3:5). When God sets you on fire in His work, that tongue, that human flame, can touch a whole neighborhood or the whole world.

We are called to be special people with the fire of God. The anointing we need to witness and to live as overcomers is found in a passion for God. Recently I heard a pastor from Russia talking about the cathedrals in his nation being turned back over to Christians. He said, "The fire of God never went out. Little groups of prayer warriors have prayed all these years." The fire sweeping the world today was preserved in basements and behind locked doors in whispered prayers.

In this mighty day of the local church raising standards in cities all over the world, the fire of God inside you will either go out, or it will consume you and release you to minister. You control the thermostat. That fire is available—moving, spreading at an uncontrollable magnitude and pace.

The day of lukewarm Christianity is coming to an end. Some Christians will wake up one day saying, "My God, where did I go wrong?" And God will answer, "I would have energized you for the work of the Kingdom, but you refused. Now you are good for nothing but to be thrown out."

Some people will be energized for a prayer watch. Some will be ground breakers for God. Some will be door keepers. God has a specific place for you in the move of the Spirit and fire sweeping the earth. God wants for His people to become "signs

141

and wonders" to a lost and dying society. When God's fire is burning, things begin to happen.

So when the passion of God is stirred, where does it go? How do we channel passion to get results? The Song of Solomon warns the lover not to stir up love before its time. God will not ignite the fire of passion within you unless He has a specific purpose to channel such enormous energy.

Some people love others as teasers who flirt with the idea of love. God is not a "teaser." God so loved the world that He gave His only begotten Son, the very best that He had. One of the major signs of God's passion in people's lives is that they begin to give to others. God wants us to love so much that we give.

I believe that God looks upon devastated cities and says to Himself, "How am I going to get the job done? How am I going to reach those who are hopeless? How am I going to teach these children what they need to know? How am I going to minister to those with diseases? How am I going to reach the rulers of nations?" And the answer is always the same. The maturing bride must move in passion until her consuming desire is to please her bridegroom.

Maturing love will cause the bride to open her ears to His voice. He will tell her, "You have a job to do. You have a task to perform."

> *"Let us be glad and rejoice and give Him glory, for the marriage of the Lamb has come, and His wife has made herself ready." And to her it was granted to be arrayed in fine linen, clean and bright, for the fine linen is the righteous acts of the saints.* (Revelation 19:7,8)

The bride of Christ makes herself ready. No one does that for her except the promptings of the Holy Spirit within—in spite of what many Christians staring into heaven believe. She is wearing her deeds—fine linen that represents her righteous acts. God is searching the earth for trustworthy, open hearts who will be the bride of Christ. This bride is passionately in love, ready to move at her bridegroom's slightest word. Her lamp is trimmed and her supply of oil is adequate. She is confident because she is intimately involved with the bridegroom. The bride of Christ is described as a city. That description interests me particularly now because God has burned such a desire in my spirit to address the condition of cities. The city of God, His bride, must become a standard to cities being wrecked by the evil and corruption of this world. A city is always composed of people, and the bride is the people of God.

The gates of the bride of Christ are open continually. Everyone is welcome inside—the rich, the poor, the lame, the weak, the brokenhearted, the successful, the failures—all may enter. This city is a refuge for those needing help. This city offers ultimate safety and security with walls built to perfection to protect everyone. The city is built solidly on the foundation of the apostles' and prophets' doctrine. The bride is a city with no temple inside her walls. Why? God and the Lamb and the saints are the temples. In fact, the glory of God is the light of that entire city. It is the same illumination that filled the Upper Room at Pentecost. The city is populated with temples where God dwells, bringing the entire city into total spiritual harmony.

People who populate this city are called "the redeemed." They are all who are saved by the blood of Christ and have overcome the grasp of the enemy through the liberating power of Christ. The redeemed include people from every nation, tribe and language on earth. They combine into one "people who were not a people" through the bloodline of Jesus Christ.

The city of God has come down from God out of His promises to His people. This city descends by proclamation. The holy city becomes reality on earth by the works of the redeemed. How? The redeemed are learning to activate their faith to receive tangible rewards from the hope realm of God. Those promises held in trust as heavenly treasures are realized on earth, as well as in eternity, by obedience to God. God loves, and God gives. As our love for Him grows, we receive His gifts to us as by-products of our love relationship.

The fire of God awakening within us is the bride's passion for the bridegroom. Rewards and benefits flow to those whose hearts burn with the passion and hunger for intimacy with the bridegroom. Christ's passion is directed toward His bride, and the result is the fire of revival sweeping the Church today. This is precisely where the Church is:

> *So when they had eaten breakfast, Jesus said to Simon Peter, "Simon, son of Jonah, do you love Me more than these?" He said to Him, "Yes, Lord; You know that I love You." He said to him, "Feed My lambs." He said to him again a second time, "Simon, son of Jonah, do you love Me?" He said to Him, "Yes, Lord; You know that I love You." He said to him, "Tend My sheep." He said to him the third time, "Simon, son of Johah, do you love Me?" Peter was grieved, because He said to him the third time, "Do you love Me?" And he said to Him, "Lord, You know all things; You know that I love You." Jesus said to*

him, *"Feed My sheep."* (John 21:15-17)

Ask yourself what the "more than these" would be if Jesus were to ask you the same question He asked Peter. Do you love Jesus more than your business? Your family? Your possessions? Your pride? Jesus' love for His bride is a love that will produce results, but the bride's love must also be pure and the primary motivation of her life.

Marriages are constantly ruined by people who love only for their own satisfaction. Intimacy becomes a physical release instead of a beautiful bonding of two lives in an eternal commitment. The beauty of spiritual intimacy in marriage allows couples to face life experiences with confidence, joy and security drawn from that strong relationship.

Jesus' response to Peter confirms the kind of love that is channeled into action. Jesus wants the love of His bride to be channeled into the work of His Kingdom. Love for the Lord is intended to ignite action in your life. Unchanneled passion is either wasted or becomes destructive. Love must be more than liking the way someone looks or dresses or walks.

Love produces action that causes you to go beyond yourself. I read a story in the *Reader's Digest* several years ago about a truck that had overturned and trapped a man underneath it. A little woman who almost couldn't lift a heavy bag of groceries lifted that truck off her husband and pulled him to safety. She felt a passion to save him. God wants you to feel that same kind of passion toward people in trouble. His love will give you the power to pull them to safety.

Beloved, let us love one another, for love is of God; and everyone who loves is born of God and knows

God. He who does not love does not know God, for God is love. In this the love of God was manifested toward us, that God sent His only begotten Son into the world, that we might live through Him. In this is love, not that we loved God, but that He loved us and sent His Son to be the propitiation for our sins. Beloved, if God so loved us, we also ought to love one another. (1 John 4:7-11)

How can the Church be so divided when we are clearly called to love one another? I began this book sharing a dream of a devastated city. Why was the city in devastation? I kept seeing the steeples of churches that were towering over that city, and a voice kept saying to me that those steeples represented the core problem of urban devastation.

Recently Andrew Young, our former mayor, U.S. Senator and representative to the United Nations under President Jimmy Carter, shared a radio talk show with me on our Wednesday night "Real Talk" session at our church. That evening, the topic was "Church and Government." Someone called in to ask him, "Why isn't government more responsive to the views of the Church on various issues?" His answer hit at the very core of the problem.

Andrew Young said, "Who is the Church? We have so many groups saying different things who claim to be speaking for the Christian community that government leaders have no clarity on who to hear!"

How can the bride of Christ be responsive corporately to her Bridegroom as long as she is so disjointed and at war with herself? Some of the greatest battles over the city of Atlanta—as in every other city—involve divisions in the Christian community. Preachers won't even sit at the table for discussion with other preachers because of doctrinal issues or organizational differences.

Meanwhile the world stands and looks and says, "My God! Is that the Church? They turn on their fallen leaders and devour them. They gossip and scheme against one another. They battle for position. They shut hurting people out unless they fit their list of those who are acceptable. Is that the Church?"

You know what I believe? I believe that someone who understands the love of God—love that casts out fear—is going to answer, "Wait just a minute. The Bride is growing up. Many are realizing even now that they are the temples of that holy city where righteousness, peace and joy dwell. Many are beginning even now to experience that baptism of fire. Many are even now beginning to feel a passion for the Bridegroom."

Someone needs to proclaim it! The bride is the standard bearer for cities! She is a city! She is making herself ready by being strong against the works of the devil. She is impassioned with the love of Christ and love for others. While she is strong against the enemy, she remembers that she must be gentle to the tender, young plants just putting out little shoots of growth. She is a protector with a mothering spirit.

And as God so loved the world that He sent His Son, Jesus Christ sends you! He will give you fire for boldness, so that those believing your testimony will have eternal life. You are becoming a city—holy, secure and filled with everlasting light. Open your gates to all who will enter! Let the fire in you give light and warmth and direction to people living in the shadows. The passion of God in you is the difference between eternal life

147

or death in people's lives and the lives of cities around the world.

8 Setting Fires Of Influence

Y ou've always had it. You have it now. Influence. You use it every day in a hundred ways you don't even realize. Many times it's not what you say as much as what you do and how you live that determines your clout.

People watch you. They see you in traffic jams and long check-out lines at the grocery store. They see you talking to your children and introducing your mother-in-law who came to visit to the neighbors living down the street.

Everything you do makes an impression. They listen to the tone of your voice. They watch where your money goes—the chairs in your house, the sandwich you ordered for lunch, your leather shoes and your new Toyota. They ask casually where you went on vacation last summer.

And you're watching them, too. You want to be an independent thinker who fits in with the majority. You try to be outstandingly average and strive to be joined to people whose values you don't agree with who surround you hour by hour all day. You feel the tension pulling constantly, pulling you between your inner and outer life.

You are a Christian living in the world that God promised to you. You've read the last chapter of the book, but you feel like a stranger on your own turf. After dinner, you hit the button on your remote control and the message flashes to your brain in living color. The world is a mess. They just don't know all that you know.

It's comforting to lock the door of your house at night. Your pillow cradles your head, and your blanket insulates you from the cold. You've prayed with your children who trust you to give them all the answers whenever they ask. Someday the time will come when you'll confess to them the only answer to get them through the darkness in the decades they will face without you, even if you live just down the street.

What makes you—in all your sameness—so different? You have bills to pay. You fight inflation by praying for that promotion at work. You think about going back to college. You want to give your children private schooling and those trendy tennis shoes they beg for. Your marriage goes through droughts, pressures, twists, turns and tempting distractions. Life could be a lot easier for everyone if only you would . . .

But, no. At your core is a fire. It ignited in Sunday School when you were ten, or at an altar at church, or in college when you were falling apart, or just before the divorce, or just before the surgery, or when you got the bad news. No matter when or how you got there, you realized you were in prison. You could have been there a long time, ever since you were born. For some reason on that memorable day, you saw the chains and the bars with total clarity.

At the time, all you were looking for was a key to get you out of jail. It all seemed too simple to really work. No one was more surprised than you. Imagine, a flame igniting at your core! Suddenly, the whole world was filled with morning sunlight, and you loved everyone in sight. You couldn't keep from smiling and smothering all the cold reactions and suspicious stares with warm embraces.

The neighbors' telling everyone that you had "flipped out" only fueled the fire. When you tried to "act normal," you just couldn't. You were flying in happiness that comes with knowing freedom for the first time in your life. Everyone needed to know about it. Life was great! They could all fly with you.

───────── Opening Up the Gifts ─────────

You started opening packages that arrived in the mail the day the fire ignited. First, the Bible. Some of it made sense, and some of it was like a poem filled with obscure symbols you simply couldn't comprehend. You were advised that it came in a variety of versions and language variations—and according to critics—some were pure, some tainted. When you asked questions about it, you discovered that people argued over which edition was the best.

No matter. You pressed through the controversy because you wanted to find out what it really said. You were shocked. The

Book wasn't religious at all. It didn't sound like most sermons or prayers. It sounded like a general ordering his troops to war. It sounded like a brilliant, aggressive strategy for world revolution. It sounded like a passionate love affair. It sounded like a father giving advice to his children with bottomless wisdom and love. But, amazingly, it did not sound religious.

And the stories in the Book were almost too honest. Every hero had skeletons in his closet—except, of course, for the fire Himself. The stories bothered you. The good guys faced peril and rejection and sometimes death for that passion at their core. They had problems you hoped you would never face. Over and over again, the lessons stressed that goodness carried a high price tag. Those promoting peace often ignited anger in others. Joy surfaced most effectively at funerals and in jail cells.

But the words of the Book both protected the fire inside you and increased its warmth. Life situations seemed to take on new meaning. Choices became more clear-cut. Just as the Book promised, a light guided your path with wisdom through the office gossip and lay-offs, the financial crisis, the illness and the family disputes.

Another package that arrived was church. You immediately recognized that you had a big problem opening it. The wrapping paper and ribbons had a confusing pattern. Twisted, knotted strings bound it up. The various parts to be assembled (according to the Book of directions) didn't fit together.

The various parts of the church seemed to be energized in a way that made the pieces resist connecting. Some divisions were based upon differences that were racial, some doctrinal, some social and political, but all emphasized with pride their reasons for the necessity of separating themselves from the other parts.

You kept comparing the Book of directions to the weekly activities of churches in your neighborhood, and you could have easily rejected the whole idea of church membership. But the Book insisted upon your exercising your covenant with God— observing the Sabbath, being baptized, partaking of communion, tithing, receiving spiritual teaching, and joining a family of believers to accomplish some common goals—so you plodded along, determined to follow directions.

Some of the churches you visited resented your enthusiasm over the inner fire. They smiled sweetly and told you that eventually you would "mature." Other churches imposed rules that the Book didn't even seem to stress as important. They made you feel that you should carry heavy tablets of stone with you everywhere you went.

The style of the services made you wonder what God really wanted from His people. Some churches deliberately abandoned all intellect and historical theology to pursue an unrestrained spiritual fervor. Other churches deliberately stifled emotions to enforce a logical, academic approach to scriptural interpretation.

With prayer and persistence, you joined a church that seemed to balance all the ingredients you needed for a productive environment. It certainly wasn't perfect. The flaws were obvious. What this church did offer was a tenderness toward God that won your trust. They didn't want to shut out people for stupid reasons. Most of the members were quick to admit their failures in honesty, but also quick to share their dreams of a better life and an eternal hope.

The leaders of this church encouraged you to channel the

energy that the inner fire produced into action. You received a menu of groups and ministries that were eager for you to join them in reaching some goals to honor the Lord. You realized that several ministries on the menu were well suited to your talents, education and skills.

Some groups emphasized service to others, some evange-lism and outreach, and some specialized in meeting the needs of administration or facilities in the daily function of the church. You found a place quickly. You felt yourself surrounded by warm, caring people who recognized your value to God and to others and were committed to helping you grow as well as growing themselves.

Prayer became a way of life for you. Those daily, hourly, moment by moment conversations with God gave you the security you had never believed to be possible. You snatched a few minutes at lunch or on break in the morning to read the Book. Your desire for fellowship with God was insatiable. You were in love.

And like a lover, you turned to David's poetry to express those deep emotions and desires. You talked with Jesus and about Jesus constantly. You wanted to please Him with every ounce of strength in your being. You wanted to look good, say the right things and think the right thoughts that would make Him happy. More than anything else, His approval was all that mattered.

Every now and then, you looked in the faces of other Christians—older, wiser, not so impassioned as you—and won-dered if you were going overboard. Had they once been as in love as you were? If so, what had happened? Had years worn away the excitement? Had the conversations and the interaction with Him become commonplace? Had they learned what to expect and couldn't believe after so long that He would provide them with wonderful surprises in life? Had their dreams been delayed for too long?

You listened closely when you talked to them. They didn't realize that you wanted answers from them to discover what you could avoid. Their stories were all different, but the killing attitude was the same. Compromise. Somewhere, somehow, it had happened.

Instead of walking in light with Him, they had chosen somewhere to step into the shadows for a moment. The shadow might have been a way to make money, or a relationship, or family demands, or vanity, or some gift from Him that they had ignored. The shadow over them was anything outside His light, any direction away from the fire.

You could not condemn them, because you realized immediately how close the shadow hovered around you—enticing, seductive and, seemingly, benevolent. The path of light was narrow with shadows on each side. Your first temptation was to want to be like them, accepted by them—solemn, unaffected, steady and emotionless. But you knew, instinctively, that such a move would quench your inner fire.

When you cried out to God, you called their names. Suddenly, you understood that you could influence not only those who didn't know Him, but also those who used to love Him stronger than now. You were beginning to recognize that your love for Him was contagious when you openly exposed others to it.

Those seemingly mature, sensible Christians could write you off initially for your youthful optimism, but deep inside the innermost recesses of their hearts—that place that didn't know time or wear and tear—they longed for that first love again. They wanted their faith to be stirred. And you could heap coals of fire upon them—simply by loving Him with all your heart, and loving them with His all-encompassing compassion.

They criticized you and trusted you at the same time. Deep within, they wanted you to succeed because your success gave them hope. They admired your sense of urgency. Your dedication to the basics—prayer, Bible study and faithful service—reminded them vaguely of a happy face in the mirror they had almost forgotten.

SPREADING THE FIRE

Meanwhile, you found out that you were magnetized. People were drawn to your voice, your smile, your touch. Your presence brought peace to the storm raging inside them. You quickly told them the secret—it wasn't you at all that attracted them and calmed their fears!

Yes, you were different! You had a fire at your core. Yes, that fire would give them the answers they needed for anything. Yes, they could have it, too, in a simple way that seemed totally illogical and ridiculous if they thought about it.

Some wanted it and others walked away—avoiding you, yet watching you closely after they learned your secret. The ones who wanted the fire understood that you were just as they were, and only He could make the difference. Soon they were asking you where you went to church, what version of the Bible you read, and when and how you spent time with the Lord each day.

Many who walked away believed that you were stronger, better and smarter than they could ever hope to be. They reasoned that you just didn't face the kind of temptations and problems that they had.

Their reaction—obviously a deception—became a warning to you. It would have been so easy to see yourself as strong and wise. Because He made you feel special, you could have believed that you were also superior. Because the help you gave really solved problems, it would have been so simple to see yourself as having "arrived" instead of one in constant need of His guard over your heart.

You didn't need many reminders to convince you that you needed that inner fire for life, but also for continuous purging. Admitting your own weaknesses and bringing them to Him made you strong in the Lord and in the power of His might. Your dependency upon Him was growing instead of diminishing. The fire needed fueling daily, or else you, like so many others, would grow dim and cold.

The honesty in your relationship with Him drew you closer. He knew all your faults, the innermost doubts and desires. He—better than anyone else including you, yourself—knew you could never make it on your own. Ironically, the dependency made you more confident and stronger in trusting Him.

Your pastor, Christian friends and other Christians in your family became your tangible support team. They humbled you when you were proud, and picked you up when you fell in exhaustion, weary in well-doing. Their love covered your weaknesses and mobilized your strengths. You became aware of how the connection with them and their prayers for you opened numerous doors to share with others. Their support increased your boldness.

———————— The Essence of the Kingdom ————————

You realized something else very important concerning your connection with other Christians. The Church is a living entity—not a shrine on the street corner of town, or another charitable institution with noble goals, or a club for fine, upstanding citizens. The Church is a blend of all kinds of people—more like a family than the house where a family lives.

Everyone arrives in God's household as a baby in great need. Salvation begins a process of training and growth leading to some great mission designed just for your particular gifts. No one in the family is meant to remain a baby. Jesus said to pray for God to send "laborers," disciples who are mature enough to know the score.

And the Church is certainly not the Kingdom of God—a government of perfection and total righteousness, peace and joy under God's rule. Not yet, anyway! Instead the Church in its imperfections—but still committed to submission to Christ—demonstrates the essence of that Kingdom to a world needing hope.

The essence of the Kingdom? Maturity teaches people that the things in life that truly matter are not the tangibles, but the intangibles. The Kingdom of God is not meat, drink, houses, land, trips or bank accounts. The Kingdom of God is righteousness, peace and joy in the Holy Spirit.

The Kingdom within you makes you to become a vessel of the Kingdom to everyone you encounter. When the fire at your core burns brightly, you bring the essence of the Kingdom of God into everyday experiences. Your willingness to do that—and sometimes the personal cost is great—will alter the dynamics of events and circumstances wherever you find yourself.

To the newborn baby, you offer prayers, snuggles and hymns to rock them to sleep. Your prayers can cover them for a lifetime. Your own babies are dedicated to God for the covering of His covenant over their lives until they make their own commitment to Him.

The babies of others open opportunities for you to remind those parents of the trust God has given to them in that precious life they hold. The overwhelming responsibility they feel can only be embraced in understanding God's love and will for that new baby's life. God sends you to remind them of His love for their child—greater than they know themselves.

You bring the essence of the Kingdom to children in answering their questions about the world around them. You point them to Jesus. You teach them to pray. You begin telling them before they understand that God made them—and all things— with a special purpose in mind. Your love convinces them of His love for them. Your peace gives them confidence and security. Your joy teaches them that life, like God, is good.

You bring the essence of the Kingdom of God to adolescents who are searching for identity. In the mountain of major choices directly in front of them, your influence becomes a deciding factor. The off-hand comment you hardly thought about when you said it could tip the scales for them in a life-determining decision.

Young people desperately need credible role models like you who will not deceive them. They need your honesty, your transparent admission of fearing failure and the wealth of experiences—sorrows, successes, regrets—that you will lay at their feet for examination. More than anything, in this time of critical self-examination, they need your love and acceptance.

You bring the essence of the Kingdom of God to any realm of education. You learned from the Book that the fear of the Lord is the beginning of knowledge. In a world of false information and propaganda, you speak the truth in love. The simplicity of your answers confounds the wisdom of this world. Whether you speak boldly against scientific theories, humanistic values, historical inaccuracies and prejudices or bondage inherent in certain political ideologies, the truth rings out loud and clear, "Be not deceived; God is not mocked."

You bring the essence of the Kingdom of God to the office, assembly line, store or marketplace. You don't play games to get ahead. You care for those under your charge. You don't lie, cheat or steal. You give an honest day's work for an honest day's pay.

Most of all, the inner fire makes you bold to your co-workers in stating who you are and what you're about. You become both a target and a refuge. You become a wall of judgment to those who reject you because of your message, and a door of life to those who meet Him because of you.

You bring the essence of the Kingdom of God to your marriage. Your treatment of your mate says so much about the day-to-day validity of your message. It makes the difference in God's answering your prayers. In marriage you have the greatest tests and the greatest rewards of Kingdom living.

God-like consistency in love, understanding and tenderness is best represented in a marriage relationship. A strong witness in this area is so important that God uses this commitment in human experience to explain Christ's love for His bride. A marriage relationship that fails to demonstrate this kind of love cannot serve as a witness of Christ's Kingdom.

Not only do you bring the essence of the Kingdom to your own marriage, but also to the marriages of others. You become sensitive to problems other couples are having, and you use your influence to strengthen their vows to one another. Older women teach younger women how to love their husbands. Older men carry tremendous influence in cautioning a young man about showing respect and faithfulness to his young wife.

With so many forces pulling husbands and wives apart, you withstand a tide of restlessness through prayer to preserve homes and restore respect and rekindle love between husbands and wives. Your commitment to family values is reflected in every decision, relationship and action.

You bring the essence of the Kingdom of God to the elderly. Many times those "golden years" do not glisten. People who once felt in control, invincible and strong may now feel vulnerable and afraid. People who view their lives as used up and worn out need to hear the good news of God's renewal.

The elderly need to experience your recognition of their value, their wisdom and their skills. They need your words of appreciation and your interest in hearing their opinions. Listen to their stories. Laugh at their jokes. They need to feel needed. And they are! Honor for the elderly provides stability for an entire society. A generational continuity provides people with a perspective of who we are, where we've come from, and where we're going.

You bring the essence of the Kingdom of God to those who are sick. You bring healing whenever you speak words of faith over those who lie in bed hour after hour, wondering if God knows or cares or whether He will ever restore them. Your joy is medicine to them. Your prayers serve as therapy in faith. Your compassion removes the guilt and condemnation and questions that sap their strength. Your love pours life into their bones and pumps healing through their veins.

You become the essence of the Kingdom to those who are dying or facing the death of a loved one. To the dying, you represent confidence of eternal life. Your presence gives them dignity because you value the life they have lived from a never-ending perspective. Your love confirms their value and contribution to this world—both now and after they are gone.

To those who have faced the death of a loved one, you weep with them as one who confirms their hope and assurance of eternity. The Comforter burning at your core gives them comfort. You don't need to debate in your mind (or even say to them) that life is not lived in vain. You know the truth. You cannot be separated from those who are joined to you through Christ. Nothing in Him is ever really lost even for a moment.

So you take the essence of the Kingdom of God with you everywhere. You are a minister on a mission for the Lord in every circumstance where you find yourself. You feel productive, confident, assured and secure. You've got it all together.

The Test

Then, when you least expect it, the sky caves in on you.

You didn't see it coming. The test. Why now? The ominous clouds by which you hoped you'd be spared engulf you. You remember praying a long time ago for God to do whatever was necessary to make you rise to your full potential in Him, but you never—in your wildest imagination—would have thought this would be required of you. Didn't God love you anymore?

Your trust is shattered. All the things you could count on disintegrate into ashes in your hands. People who respected you turn away. Those closest to you touch you with sterile gloves like one brought in from surgery to an intensive care unit. You hear the whispers as you walk by. Inside is a gash, a pain, a stab wound that should have killed you that will not stop bleeding. You know that even if you could somehow, possibly, someday be healed, the scar will remain forever.

You contemplate death like never before. Something inside you has certainly died. Was it your love for Him? No. Strangely, that love is greater than you felt in the early days. Was it His plan for your life? No. Things will not be as you had thought, but you can see in an astounding way—that you would never have believed if someone had told you—how His plan that He whispered to you is going to happen.

So what has died? Finally, you understand! Death to your subtle reliance upon yourself. Death to your reliance upon your good looks, your charm, your intelligence, your charisma. Death to your keen ability to figure it all out. Now all that is gone. The test burned it out of you as no lesson in the classroom could. You had to experience personally the rejection, the contradictions, the accusations—the fellowship of His suffering. Didn't you pray to know Him?

Now the power of His resurrection isn't only for Him; it's for your life today. You are raised from the dead to new life. Now you bear the weight of your cross. Now you share wounds in your hands and in your side where the blood flows out of you. Didn't you ask Him for this close understanding of His heart?

Didn't you tell Him you were willing to be sacrificed—the fellowship of His suffering?

After the test—which leaves an ugly scar and a limp in your walk, and questions in every face and in every voice you encounter from that day forward—God will trust you. He trusted Himself to guard you closely until now in controlled circumstances. Now He still guards you, but you are different. You don't question the crazy route you are taking toward His throne. Nothing makes sense anymore except to walk where He tells you to go.

The fire at your core is roaring. It consumes all the criticism, praises, curses or applause given to you in His behalf. Others' opinions no longer matter. Love for others is intensified by that consuming fire. All of your life is played out to Him—an audience of One. But millions also watch in hope and expectation.

Now you see the big picture. You and hundreds and thousands like you are sent on a mission. It's all for the millions of spiritually starving souls that you have been blessed, empowered, honored, stripped and raised from the dead! You, the Church, have food for them. You feed them with His body. His blood is poured out for the remission of their sins. When the hungry discover that you have food, they flock to you continually. You feed the lambs because you love Him. You become their light through the dark nights.

You finally know who you are. You are the Church of Jesus Christ, His empowered bride. You've grown to stand as a comparable mate for Him. You do not flinch at the chaotic whirlwind surrounding you. Every day kingdoms rise and fall. The stock market fluctuates at every news event. War rages. Rumors of national uprisings abound. The earth trembles upon its axis. Nature is infuriated with all creatures on the planet and conspires to destroy them. Politicians debate the issues. Terrorism. Famine. Deception. Heart failure. Death.

But the Church stands firmly planted. You do not tremble or shake. You are not afraid at hearing the latest news bulletin that interrupted the regularly scheduled broadcast. You know the end of the matter. Your bridegroom is coming for His bride. The time for the wedding draws near. Your hope chest overflows with the best gifts a bride can have.

The voice of the Church is amplified around the world in ways you could have never imagined. God's master marketing strategy takes your comments into every household in every nation via satellite. You are unafraid to face the storm of opposition growing against you because your words cut like a sword. People choose sides according to their readiness to hear what you have to say. Pharaoh's forces are outraged at your audacity.

But the fire burns higher and brighter. The light intensifies inside you and around you and upon you, filling the earth. Darkness cannot overpower the brightness of your light. And you, the Church, the bride who is prepared with great anticipation, lift up your head and cry with words at last shattering the barrier between flesh and spirit, "Come! Lord Jesus, come!"

ABOUT THE AUTHOR

Bishop Earl Paulk is senior pastor of Chapel Hill Harvester Church located in Atlanta, Georgia. Chapel Hill has twenty-two full-time pastors serving a parish of approximately twelve thousand people, with thousands more receiving ministry by television and other outreach.

Bishop Paulk grew up in a classical Pentecostal family as the son of Earl P. Paulk, Sr., a former assistant general overseer in the Church of God. His grandfather, Elisha Paulk, was a Freewill Baptist preacher. Earl Paulk began his ministry at age seventeen as a student at Furman University, a Baptist institution. Along with a Bachelor of Arts degree in history from Furman, he earned a Master of Divinity degree from Candler School of Theology at Emory University, a Methodist seminary. In 1987, he received a Doctorate of Theology degree from Oral Roberts University. In 1990, he received a Doctorate of Divinity degree from the New Covenant International Bible College in New Zealand. Personal and educational exposure have given Bishop Paulk an ecumenical understanding enjoyed by few church leaders in the world today.

Earl Paulk was named to the office of Bishop in the International Communion of Charismatic Churches in 1982. The ICCC provides covering for thousands of churches worldwide. Bishop Paulk directly serves hundreds of networking churches throughout the U.S., Latin America, Canada, Mexico and South Africa. He serves on the governing boards of Charismatic Bible Ministries and Network of Christian Ministries. He is a regent at Oral Roberts University.

Besides his own weekly television program, "The Cathedral at Chapel Hill," Bishop Paulk is an internationally-known speaker and the author of fifteen books. He is a frequent guest on talk shows, which include "Larry King Live," "Richard Roberts," and numerous other television and radio talk shows which discuss specific issues.

A March 1990 issue of **Christianity Today** on "Megachurches" listed Chapel Hill Harvester Church as one of the ten largest churches in the United States. Chapel Hill's ministries include human service ministries such as support groups to the chemically addicted, *Challenge* for those affected by homosexualtiy, ministry to single parents, Literacy classes, *Super Saints* for senior citizens, *New Order* for young married couples and singles, a ministry to AIDS patients, programs for those living in two inner-city government-subsidized housing communities, a multi-faceted pastoral counseling service and many others.

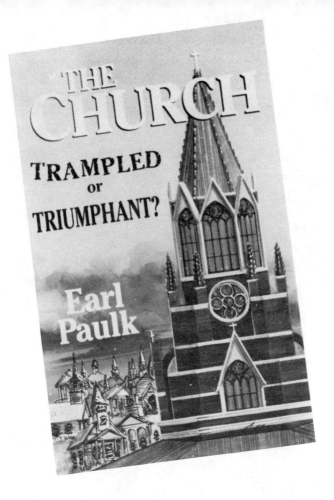

Is the modern Church trampled beyond repair, or is the
Church triumphant in offering society solutions and
direction for the 21st Century? Earl Paulk insists that the
Church has not become as salt without flavor, good for
nothing but to be trampled under the foot of public
opinion and media ridicule. Instead, Earl Paulk issues a
proclamation of hope. The fire of this proclamation will
ignite Christians who sit passively behind sanctuary
walls. And for people searching for solutions, it's a
proclamation worth considering.

Order form, see page 177

101 Questions Your Pastor Hopes You Never Ask!

OOPS!! But they did ask...

... about AIDS, sex, drugs, cults, alcohol, homosexuality, teenagers, dancing...

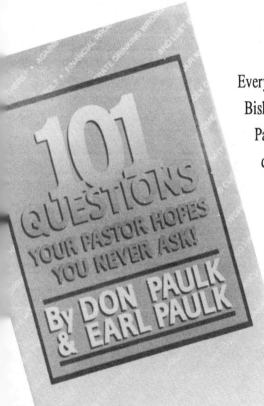

Every Wednesday evening Bishop Earl Paulk and Pastor Don Paulk field life's most difficult questions from their 10,000+ congregation, as well as a live radio audience. No subject is off limits, no topic is left unanswered.

Chances are, if you've had a question you were too embarrassed to ask...
it's in there!

Order form, see page 177

Anyone can see symptoms. But it takes the eye of a physician to see the infirmity... and the skill of a surgeon to cut it away.

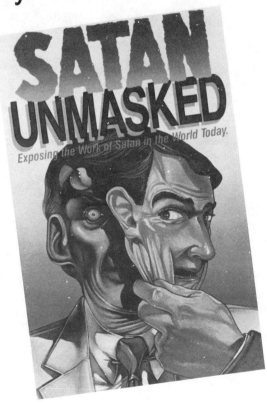

In this penetrating look at the patterns of evil, Earl Paulk exposes the blatant attacks against you and your family. And he delves beneath the surface to confront even the subtlest strategies meant to keep you from changing the world you live in.

Order form, see page 177

SEX
IS GOD'S IDEA
EARL PAULK

THIS BEST-SELLER IS RATED "R"...

... for "real." It's real because it's frank, funny and sensitive.

And because it takes sex out of the bedroom and dares to mix it with the rest of life. If you've been looking for a primer on healthy relationships to share with your whole family, or if you're ready to take the next step in intimacy with your beloved, *Sex Is God's Idea* is a great idea for you.

Order form, see page 177

Kingdom Publishers

P.O. Box 7300 • Atlanta, GA 30357

Name _____

Address _____

City _____ State _____ Zip_____

Telephone (___) _____

QTY.	TITLE		PRICE	AMT.
	The Local Church Says, "Hell, No!"	*Earl Paulk*	9.95	
	101 Questions Your Pastor Hopes You Never Ask *hardcover*	*Don Paulk & Earl Paulk*	$12.95	
	The Church: Trampled or Triumphant?	*Earl Paulk*	9.95	
	20/20 Vision – A Clear View on the Kingdom of God	*Earl Paulk*	2.50	
	Sex Is God's Idea	*Earl Paulk*	7.95	
	Satan Unmasked	*Earl Paulk*	9.95	
	Spiritual Megatrends	*Earl Paulk*	8.95	
	I Laugh, I Cry *hardcover*	*Don Paulk*	12.95	
	Discerning Spirits *(4-tape series)*	*Earl Paulk & Lynn Mays*	20.00	
	Please send me your latest Kingdom Publishers Catalog FREE		FREE	FREE
		Total	$2.00	
		Postage & Handling		
		TOTAL DUE		

Enclose check or money order for full amount
and mail along with this order form to:

Post Office Box 7300
Atlanta, Georgia 30357